WARRIORS, WORKERS, WHINERS, & WEASELS

TIM O'LEARY

WARRIORS, WORKERS, WHINERS, & WEASELS

Understanding and Using
the Four Personality Types to Your Advantage

XEPHOR
P R E S S

XEPHOR
P R E S S

Xephor Press
3 Holly Hill Lane
Katonah, NY 10536
www.xephorpress.com
1-914-232-6708

ISBN 0-9752638-6-2

Printed and bound in the United States of America.

Library of Congress Cataloging-in-Publication Data

O'Leary, Tim.
Warriors, workers, whiners, and weasels : the 4 personality types in business and how to manage them to your advantage / by Tim O'Leary.
    p. cm.
    ISBN 0-9752638-6-2 (hardcover : alk. paper)
    1. Psychology, Industrial. 2. Organizational behavior. 3. Personality.
I. Title.
HF5548.8.O49 2006
658.3001'9—dc22

2005032049

TABLE OF CONTENTS

AUTHOR'S NOTES

It was late spring—1971 or 1972. I'd risen at 5 A.M. and ridden my bike three miles to Central Park for Little League tryouts. The field was covered with nervous kids and volunteer coaches none too happy about being there at 6 in the morning. And I spied one lone figure sitting in the stands. My father, dressed in a suit and short-brimmed hat, chomping on a cigar even before breakfast, the only father among the hundred or so kids on the field to brave the early hour, was there—as he always was. Never to interfere or pass judgment, he was always standing in the wings to support, discipline, entertain, and instruct by example. And when paired with my mother, they were the perfect team to teach me much of what I write about in this book. As they celebrate their sixty-eighth year of marriage, I continue to learn new lessons about patience, family, and love from both of them.

Much later in life I was fortunate enough to meet someone else who continues to shape me. My beautiful wife Michelle is really the coauthor of this book. The definition of a Warrior, she is my biggest advocate and most constructive critic, and I love our love affair.

Finally, the string of events and relationships that leads to a book. My friends Bill Waite and Glen Timmons introduced me to my agents Richard Hill and Greg Link, who introduced me to my publisher Xephor Press and Tom Woll, who introduced me to my editor Ruth Mills, and this is the result. My thanks to all of you.

PART ONE

Recognizing the Four Personality Types

"Boss Hawg" and the Budding Warrior: How I Learned About Warriors, Workers, Whiners, and Weasels

> "Try not to become a man of success but rather
> to become a man of value."
> —Albert Einstein

I started my first company when I was sixteen years old, and accordingly, I got an early introduction to the world of Warriors, Workers, Whiners, and Weasels. A student organization to which I belonged was constantly lamenting the fact that there was no place for restless, hormone-laden teenagers to go on Friday and Saturday nights in our Montana town. (At least, no place that didn't involve consuming massive quantities of keg beer in remote locations while singeing our hair next to a bonfire.) Rather than simply lament our plight, we took the Warrior's approach (got a problem, find a solution) which led to the idea of a teen-age dance club.

The project was initially welcomed with open arms by parents, the high schools, and city officials. Dancing in a supervised setting certainly seemed like a good alternative to the other potential activities teenagers might pursue. The city was even quick to offer vacant warehouse space to house the club, which we christened "The Fourth Floor Alley" to commemorate its location and alley entrance. The local newspaper provided financial support, local contractors offered free time and materials to renovate the space, and a graphic designer even produced a logo for the new club. Perhaps most important, a local electrical company threw in a mirrored ball to hang above the dance floor. For the first time, I experienced firsthand the value and importance of having a pool of dedicated Warriors to conceive an idea and sell it through, and Workers willing to see the plan to fruition.

I was put in charge of the new organization, and my friends and I quickly went to work to open our new nightclub. Of course, my motives were not all charitable. Although a teen dance club was a great idea, the thought of me running it was an even better concept. At sixteen, you seek any power base you can find, and managing a dance club seemed like an ideal way to meet members of the opposite sex.

We worked many long hard hours getting The Fourth Floor Alley ready to open. I spent the afternoons soliciting donations from local businesses, and I soon had enough mismatched tables, chairs, and glasses committed to make the place look like a real club. The local beverage distributor, a good friend of my dad's, even donated a soft-drink fountain. Everything was coming together, and in a couple weeks, The Fourth Floor Alley would open. At least, that's what I thought—until I got the call.

On a Friday afternoon, I was summoned to the mayor's office. The mayor had been a great supporter of the project, milking the positive publicity for all it was worth, and I surmised he was calling to give me more good news—perhaps the city was going to donate parking space or a sound system to our new enterprise. The mayor's assistant seated me outside his office while the mayor finished a phone call, and because the door was slightly ajar, I couldn't help but hear his side of the conversation. Now mind you, I wasn't purposely eavesdropping (that would be a Weasel thing to do)—but given the mayor's elevated tone of voice, hearing him was unavoidable.

Much to my dismay, the conversation was confirming the demise of

The Fourth Floor Alley. "I know we promised these damn kids the space, but we got the library-expansion funding and I need to put more city offices up there. Hell, I didn't want a bunch of long-haired little kids running around the building anyway," I heard the somewhat ruby-necked mayor exclaim. (Keep in mind, this was the mid-1970s, when having hair extending past your collar in Montana most likely meant you were an escaped family member of the Manson clan.) "I'll come up with some excuse. I'll just blame the lawyers."

A few minutes later, I was summoned into his chambers, with the mayor unaware I had heard his conversation. With a great show of flourish and regret, he explained to me that he was canceling our dance club because the city attorney was concerned about liability issues. "I really wanted to do this thing, Tim," he said, with his most earnest look. "I really think it is a great thing, and I believed in what you were doing. I really went to the mat for you on this deal, but the legal boys just say no-can-do. You know how those damn lawyers are. We can't risk a big lawsuit if one of you kids gets hurt. I'm really sorry, son, but there's nothing more I can do." He concluded with his best "it's-the-system-we-live-with" shrug.

Of course, he neglected to mention the fact that he also had committed the space to an office expansion, sold us down the river, and actually considered us long-haired little shits.

WHAT I LEARNED FROM THIS EARLY WEASEL EXPERIENCE

I didn't know it at the time, but I was having my first business encounter with a Weasel. In the course of this book, I will talk a lot about Weasels—how to spot them, how to handle them, the best way to dry-clean your suit after contact with one, and how to keep your business and life as Weasel-free as possible. But at sixteen, I was learning the cardinal rules of business the hard way—*never trust a Weasel, and Weasels lurk everywhere.* Of course, it may be self-evident to say, "Don't trust a Weasel," but the challenge often becomes identifying the true Weasels. More on this later.

This was a defining moment in my life and not just because I had confronted my first business Weasel (and isn't it interesting that the Weasel would be a politician). It was also important because of the way I responded. "That's not true," I blurted at the mayor. "I heard you talking on the phone, and you said you were giving the space away for offices. And you called us long-haired little kids! You don't care anything about the project."

I didn't realize it, but at that moment I had taken the first step to becoming a Warrior. A Worker or a Whiner most likely would have crept out of the mayor's office, afraid to confront the situation. The Whiner then would have complained later to others that have no control over the situation.

My response might not have been the smartest way to handle the problem. Mayors are not accustomed to being, nor do they like to be, challenged by mouthy sixteen-year-old eavesdroppers. But one of the tenets of being a Warrior is to confront Weasels head on. They are like the suspicious mole that you get removed from your skin because it may signal an invasion of your body by a life-threatening cancer. Left to his own devices, a Weasel may bring disease and ultimately death to you, your career, or your company. My instincts, even at sixteen, were correct: confront Weasels when you first discover them. Let them know you know their true colors. Weasels, by their very nature, fear confrontation, because they exist in a world of insecurity and deception. Of course, this works better for adults confronting adults. Hiz Honor was not about to be pushed around by a sixteen-year-old wannabe Warrior, and he blew up like Boss Hawg at a Duke Brothers' birthday party.

"You've been listening to my private conversations, boy!" he screamed. This is a classic Weasel response: shift the blame. "How dare you. I could have you arrested for that!" Another Weasel technique: threaten the improbable or impossible. There was little point in arguing anymore with the mayor, so I listened to his tirade for a few minutes, and somewhat in shock, I left City Hall, my nightclub dream shattered by a Weasel and city politics.

I walked the two blocks to *The Gazette*, found a reporter who had been covering the development of The Fourth Floor Alley for the paper, and related the entire story, including the fact that I had heard the mayor refer to my group as "long-haired little shits." The reporter, most likely hard up for anything that resembled controversy in our city, was hot on the story. She wrote an article on the demise of the club, taking a sympathetic approach. The article received great placement in the Sunday paper. Bright and early Sunday morning, I received a phone call at home from the mayor, who used a variety of expletives normally not directed at sixteen-year-olds by major public officials.

Unfortunately, we didn't get our dance club, and I was no longer welcome around City Hall, but I did get a painful but valuable introduction into what has developed into an entire philosophy that I now live by. To be successful, you need to understand your own motivations, talents, and ethics—and the motivations, talents, ethics, and limitations of everyone with whom you work. Warriors constantly challenge their own limitations, pushing themselves to go further and achieve more than they think possible. They also learn to control their environment as much as possible via an understanding of themselves and those whom they impact, and those who can potentially impact their environment.

Warriors utilize a variety of personal tools that help them achieve their goals and sleep soundly at night. Great Warriors ultimately live and die by the credibility they establish through their actions, and one of the most painful and ongoing lessons in their lives is that most people don't share their devotion to keeping their word and telling the truth.

HOW THIS EXPERIENCE HELPED ME IN MY CAREER—AND HOW IT CAN HELP YOU IN YOURS

Like most Warriors, I discovered my passion early in life. I have been a proud and rabid entrepreneur since I was old enough to ask for the sale. I discovered early that there is nothing better than the feeling of developing your own plan, doing the deal, and seeing it all come together successfully.

Since graduating from college, I have never really had a job working for anyone except myself for any extended period of time. Perhaps this speaks volumes of my own arrogance, independence, or inability to accept a higher order, but I have always insisted on controlling my own destiny. I personally love the early stages of a business, when expectations, energy levels, and risk are at their highest point. I have spent my career conceptualizing and starting companies, and selling my ideas. My endeavors have ranged from tiny to significant enterprises: an industrial manufacturing company, a computer software company, vending machines, a limousine service, a catalog, a major Internet retailer, television production companies, a marketing consulting firm, an entertainment company, and advertising agencies. I've learned wonderful and hard lessons working with partners, investors, venture capital companies, private equity firms, and banks.

I've watched and assisted companies in growing from the idea stage to hundreds of millions in sales in short periods, and I've had the pleasure of meeting and working with many world-class entrepreneurs and business managers (and unfortunately a few world-class Weasels). I've worked with celebrities who range from one-hit wonders to some of the biggest in the history of entertainment. I've also spent time in the boardrooms of some of the world's largest corporations, often in wonderment that these mega-companies survive, given the anti-productive business cultures filled with Whiners, Weasels, and the fearful and misdirected Workers they have created. I love to surround myself with talented entrepreneurs (other Warriors and Workers), and to see a business idea into successful fruition.

Like most Warriors, I have frequently failed. Some of the companies I've started have been unsuccessful and gone out of business due to my own inexperience, impatience, occasional incompetence, or the fact that they were simply poorly conceived or executed. I've also made a lot of money successfully navigating industries that are often thought to be Weasel hotbeds (can you say infomercial?). Through this education process, I have sometimes let my own integrity lapse, allowed my arrogance to take me down the wrong paths, treated good people badly, misman-aged my employees, and made other mistakes (some of which I unfortu-nately keep making). I constantly hope I learn enough from the experiences to prevent repeating the same mistakes too often.

HOW TO RECOGNIZE
THE FOUR PERSONALITY TYPES

Perhaps the biggest lesson I have learned is that building successful com-panies and relationships requires the traits of the Warrior (and the proper use of the Warrior's tools): a combination of never-ending personal drive and confidence, integrity, innovation, intuition, and, most important, the ability to fill the organization with the right mixture of people. After hir-ing, firing, and observing hundreds of employees, I have found that com-panies are populated by four distinct personalities, which I have christened Warriors, Workers, Whiners, and Weasels. Most companies of significant size have a mixture of all four, as it is almost impossible to build a large staff without having a cross-section. Smaller companies are especially vulnerable to having the wrong mix. It's integral to hold on to your Warriors and Workers. And one too many Whiners or Weasels can topple an organization in no time.

WARRIORS

Successful companies need at least one Warrior—the aggressive innovator who conceptualizes and defines the organization and who fights the tough battle to make it successful. Some companies have many Warriors, which can sometimes make for really great organizations or, in other cases, can lead to disaster, depending on whether or not the Warriors can work together. Often, successful companies fail or enter a long downward spiral when the Warrior exits and allows the company to be run by Workers, Weasels, and Warrior-wannabes.

Warriors and budding Warriors tend to share certain attributes. Warriors are sometimes not the most pleasant people to be around. Although they are usually charming and invigorating, they are also usually self-centered, intolerant, hot-tempered, domineering, highly critical, and often driven to the point of seeming distraction. Great Warriors may be painful to work for, but they more than compensate for their shortcomings by spreading success and by living with a devout respect for relationships.

On the plus side, though, their hallmark is their self-confidence. Optimism comes naturally to Warriors. They always assume they will be successful, because they understand that they ultimately control their own destiny. Warriors know there is nobody better to depend on than themselves, and if the plan doesn't work out, they are equally willing to take the blame.

Warriors love selling and innately understand that selling themselves is more important than selling the product or service they represent. They are not afraid to ask for the order, the raise, the promotion, a date, a better table at a restaurant, a discount, an upgrade to first class, or a bigger hotel room. Warriors understand that almost everything is negotiable, and the big question is whether or not one has the drive to ask for what you want, and the finesse to get it. Another important Warrior trait is their seeming inability to give up. Warriors often win just because they are willing to stay in the battle longer and endure more to ultimately succeed.

WORKERS

The backbone of any company is the Worker—the dependable soldiers who take direction from the Warriors and make things happen. Great companies always have great Workers. It is certainly possible for a great Worker to become a Warrior, though it isn't healthy for all of a company's Workers to be aspiring Warriors. There is tremendous honor and value in just being a Worker.

Workers understand their essential role in society, and they also tend to live the most balanced life among the four categories. Great Workers take tremendous pride in their craft, be it building jets, answering phones, driving a truck, designing microchips, writing legal briefs, or managing a large staff. Workers come in every shape, size and economic category; they perform duties that range from the mundane to the complex.

Being a Worker is not a badge of social stature or intelligence, and Workers are in no way inferior to Warriors. They simply occupy a different and equally important place in the big scheme of things. They tend to be a contented lot, having mastered the balance of career, lifestyle, and the outside activities they enjoy. And they also share some of the attributes of the Warrior. They take responsibility for their actions and pride in their achievements. They always strive to be the best they can be, and to be acknowledged as "best in category" at whatever they do. They are team players and understand the concept of "loving the one you're with" to collectively achieve success. They are the support system that almost all Warriors require to be successful.

WHINERS

Certainly, we have all experienced the Whiner in a workplace. Whiners might be competent workers, but their negativity and dissatisfaction overshadow their performance. Often, their whining is a mask for their incompetence. They spend a disproportionate amount of time complaining about others and blaming everyone else for their personal lack of success. They usually attempt to recruit more Whiners from the workplace, creating dissatisfaction among the Workers.

Often, Whiners are Warrior-wannabes. Sadly enough, they are frequently talented, possessing many Warrior attributes, with the exception of some of the most important Warrior traits: self-responsibility and respect for relationships. Warriors know that if they fail, the failure belongs to them, regardless of the circumstances of the failure. Whiners take the opposite approach. Anything bad that happens is someone else's fault. They occupy the victim's seat in business and life, and they find it easy to turn on their friends if they need to shift blame.

One of their great pleasures in life is to contemplate and spread other's troubles (hence they tend to be big gossipers), as it provides a welcome distraction from their obsession with their own perceived problems. Though you occasionally meet people who have been ingrained Whiners from birth, it is normally a process one goes through that culminates by the time someone is in his or her mid-20s. It is important for parents and managers to observe those who are adopting Whiner traits so they can perhaps be turned before they make the final transition.

Whiners are innately critical of everyone but themselves and cynical of everything around them. They manage to find a problem even with good news, and like a spreading parasite, they seek to convert the contented around them into Whiners.

WEASELS

Finally, we meet the Weasel. Weasels are always negative, personally and professionally. They operate from a profound sense of insecurity that clouds their existence and drives them to destroy, for the strangely misguided sense of fulfillment it provides them. They have no regard for honesty, relationships, long-term credibility, or friendships. Perhaps they came from sad and tragic backgrounds, and their stories may leave you filled with pity. Or maybe they just popped up from the wrong side of the gene pool. But they are cancer to a relationship or company. And like cancer, they are also clever at disguising themselves. I've worked with people for months, even years, believing them to be competent Workers or even Warriors, before discovering they were Weasels of the worst kind.

The saddest thing about most Weasels is that they are typically talented people, but because they are driven by insecurity, they choose to concentrate on negativity instead of succeeding based on their talents. Through early identification of Weasel-like traits, one might be able to stop an impressionable young person from degrading into a Weasel. It is essential to develop strong Weasel radar to keep your company healthy and happy.

Weasels tend to be strong in personality, which can make them difficult to identify at the onset. They may initially appear to be a Warrior or Worker. But the core trait of a Weasel is to instill confusion and distrust within his or her structure. Trace back a nasty rumor mill, and usually there was a Weasel involved in its initial development. Weasels delight in stirring up trouble between factions, fueling it with distrust, rumors, and outright lies. They will claim to be everyone's friend, while not honoring any friendship. Every motivation they possess is designed to fill their internal void, and true friendship is almost impossible for them to attain.

Due to their aggressive personalities and relentless methods, they can often become successful and achieve positions of power. And there is nothing tougher than dealing with a Weasel-controlled business. They constantly find reasons to berate those they work with and avoid paying their bills and other obligations. Weasels take great delight in the perception that they have taken some advantage or won some battle—even if their opponent did not realize they were in a competition.

HOW THIS BOOK CAN HELP YOU

In the following pages, I will detail these four personality types, and I suspect you will find yourself (if you aren't already) classifying your co-workers, your family, and yourself. This simple classification system will help you understand the dynamics of what is happening around you, improve your position within your organization, and advance your personal development and clarify your decisions.

If you are already a Warrior, defining these personality types will help you understand yourself, appreciate those attributes that may have sometimes troubled you, and perhaps make you even more successful. You will understand the "Warrior Tools" that have helped make you a Warrior and learn how to utilize them even better. Understanding these attributes also may help you develop those around you. Perhaps you have budding Warriors in your household or company who could use a boost.

If you are a Worker or a Whiner who aspires to be a Warrior, take heart; this book will help you identify the personality traits that are keeping you from becoming all you can be, give you the tools you need to develop to be successful, or at the very least give you satisfaction in the life you have chosen.

And if you are a Weasel, well, all I can say is—be very, very careful. We're on to you!

I have organized the book into six sections. Section 1 provides an overview the four personality types and how they typically interact. Subsequent sections drill down into the world of Warriors, Workers, Whiners, and Weasels to help identify their traits and characteristics. Chapter 6, "The Warrior's Toolbox: Ten Tools Every Warrior Should Possess," is the longest in the book, because it details specific action steps for improvement.

Throughout the book, I've included tips, case studies, and drills to help build positive traits in yourself and others, and rid your environment of the negativity and problems that Whiners and Weasels carry. And you also will find "Recipes for Failure"—mini-chapters that detail the most common self-destructive behaviors that should be avoided or corrected at all costs.

For additional case studies, drills, updates on some of the good work Warriors and Workers are doing, a Warriors and Weasels blog, the nominating area for your favorite Warriors and Weasels, the "Weasel Alert" section, and many other features, visit www.warriorsandweasels.com.

. . . .

In the next chapter, we'll delve deeper into how "The Four W's" can help you understand yourself and your motivations better.

CHAPTER 2

"But Of Course, I'm a Warrior": How to Become What You Really Want to Be

"If at first you don't succeed—try to hide your astonishment."
—Harry F. Banks

I n the following pages, I am going to introduce you to a philosophy that I live by in life and in business. "The Four W's," as I call this belief system, is a classification process: a simple checklist that allows me to understand myself and the people I work with better. Through this understanding, I find personal motivation, make better decisions, and eliminate much of the angst individuals so often feel when faced with people-related issues. It has made me a better manager in my business and my personal life. It's made me happier. It's helped me build successful companies, have better business and personal relationships, grow wealthy, and understand myself better.

Much of it is self-evident—e.g., it is certainly better to be a Warrior or a Worker than a Whiner or a Weasel. But at a deeper level, I find that the beauty of the The Four W's is its simplicity. Success in business and in life is really not all that complicated; it is simply a process of coming to terms with yourself and taking a long-term and realistic approach toward your life and your career. Establish your goals and a plan of action, build a positive personal brand, and take responsibility for your own actions. Expand your positive attributes, and work to eliminate those that are holding you back. Work toward a desired outcome, and don't expect it to happen by itself. And ideally, you must also understand and utilize the talents of those around you, and realize the warning signs of those who can bring dysfunction and failure into your life. Finally, put it all together so that it enhances everything you do. Your work and life should happily coexist, and getting up in the morning should be a pleasure and an adventure.

WHY THIS BOOK IS NEEDED *NOW*

The new millennium has signaled a kind of Weasel renaissance, the likes of which we have not seen for years! The despicable and shifty ferrets have bred and multiplied, and they now swarm the earth like well-fed and organized fire ants, working their way up and down the food chain, and leaving scorched, barren ground in their wake. They have embedded themselves in our social, political, and corporate cultures at the highest levels, making corruption, manipulation, and outright deceit more the rule than the exception.

Weasel behavior is so common now that instead of immediately condemning it, we have come to expect it, sometimes even embrace it, lowering our expectations of our fellow man. Our tolerance level for the selfish, lying, destructive, and sometimes deadly habits of Weasels has risen to a point that should cause us all concern about the coming years. Weasels are wearing us down, often winning the battle due to society's hesitation to hold ourselves to a higher standard and the easy temptations that Weasels use as recruiting tools.

- *We are told that success and money are our God-given rights and that almost anyone might achieve enormous wealth and success almost by accident.* The end justifies the means, so go ahead and do whatever it takes to get what you want. Who cares about ethics and credibility? Acquiring the most "bling bling" is the objective.

- *Everyone deserves to be famous.* We worship at the altar of the celebrity, where fame based on talent has been replaced by infamy at any cost. Magazines and newspaper headlines seldom feature inspirational accounts of people improving society; instead, we get to know the intimate and lurid life details of accused murderers and celebrity criminals. In this vapid world that offers "fifteen minutes of fame" for anyone willing to sufficiently demean or expose themselves, our hometown heroes are not honored for *positive achievements.* Attention goes to those willing to let cameras photograph their most personal moments, go on national television and consume insects, have themselves locked in boxes filled with snakes, marry people they have spent a total of twenty minutes getting to know, or have themselves surgically altered to the point they are unrecognizable by their friends and family.

- *Live the "lottery lifestyle."* Simply answer the door and Ed McMahon might be standing there, ready to present you with an oversized check that will change your life! Drop all your life savings into one Internet stock so you can become a billionaire. Go ahead and live well past your financial means. Charge that credit card to the max, take out second and third mortgages, live like a rock star, and somehow it will all work out.

We are bombarded with media and marketing messages that imply that some unknown force owes us happiness and success, and that by simply calling a toll-free number, answering simplistic questions, or registering a URL, we will make it all come true. The media wants us to believe—and we are anxious to accept—the concept that wealth, success, and happiness are God-given rights, and that anytime, by the simple luck of the draw, it may come to us, despite the fact that your odds of winning the lottery are roughly equivalent to being hit by a meteor!

Well, you won't find that message in this book. Just as I don't try to time the stock market, I also don't believe in leaving my success or happiness to chance. Although in America, we are guaranteed the right to *pursue* happiness, nowhere are we guaranteed to *achieve* it. If you want to be successful, happy, and/or potentially wealthy, it is *your responsibility* to take action. That is a core message of this book.

In many ways, "The Four W's" idea is also a throwback to the forgotten and simplistic philosophies that governed our parents and grandparents.

Remember "a man is only as good as his word" and the other homespun theories of life and business? Well, despite the fact that they were often forgotten in the wake of the "Gordon Gekko Go-Go 80s," quickly followed by the "Enron Internet Generation" of the last decade, it is still good advice. Credibility, along with honesty and other dependable traits, are core attributes of the Warrior.

HOW THIS BOOK CAN HELP YOU BECOME WHAT YOU REALLY WANT TO BE

When you first saw this book, you probably looked at the title, and immediately thought: "But of course, I'm a Warrior—what else could I possibly be?" And accordingly, you bought the book for one of the following reasons:

1. You wanted just to make sure.

2. You hoped to learn techniques that will allow your Warrior traits to come forth and shine.

3. You suffer at the hands of Whiners and Weasels all the time, and you figured this book might offer some relief.

4. You plan to give this book as a gift to your favorite creep at the office, signed anonymously, "to the world's biggest Weasel, from one of the many who detest you." (Or perhaps you received the book anonymously with a similar inscription, which really has you wondering . . .)

First of all, if you have chosen reason number four, keep in mind that a Warrior would never act anonymously. The Warrior would waltz into the Weasel's office, slam this book down on his or her desk, and proclaim loudly, "Here, I made the assumption you could read, so I bought you a little something that might help improve your career and generally dismal outlook on life, you pathetic little Weasel."[1]

---

1. Keep in mind it is always a good idea to avoid physical altercations at the office, even with Weasels. Although most Weasels will hide under their desks or run to the restroom at the first sign of a confrontation, there is always the risk of encountering a rabid, dangerous Weasel. You wouldn't want to end up with a Bic pen sticking out of your neck.

Or, I hope you bought this book with a little more of an open mind. You might be seeking to improve yourself, and you're curious what classification your really fall into. Remember that you don't necessarily need to be a Warrior to be fulfilled. There is great satisfaction in being a Worker, especially if you have eliminated the angst of trying to achieve something that doesn't suit you. The key is to fully utilize your talents, while finding peace within yourself, and that is what "The Four W's" idea is all about.

This book is a tool to sort out the positive and negative personality types that we all possess, hopefully allowing you to start an honest internal assessment about your own talents, hopes, and dreams. With that information in mind, this book also will help you develop the tools to reach your goals.

Often, the dividing point between being a Warrior and a Worker is simply deciding on the balance of what you are willing to sacrifice. I know many talented individuals who could easily transform themselves from Worker to Warrior status, but that would involve changing their positive personal and family lives—a step that they quite justifiably refuse to take. This balancing act between home and work can sometimes take a negative tack and transform a Worker into a Whiner. I've met many Workers who were unwilling to make the hard choices and who expect to take a Warrior's position without the sacrifices it entails. Because Warrior status is earned, not given, these Workers are constantly unhappy, because they crave something they can't have. Filled with bitterness, and unable to accept responsibility for their inability to fully find comfort in their classification, they become Whiners, blaming everyone else for their position. What a waste of talent.

If you are destined to be a Warrior and if you will only be happy once you have attained Warrior status, the only thing holding you back might be a few minor changes in attitude, which The Four W's will help you understand. Whiners are seldom happy; but most people who fall into this category don't even realize they are Whiners. The Four W's will help Whiners face their dissatisfaction and make the changes that will ultimately transform them into happier and healthier people. And in this politically correct age, we often feel guilty about confronting the "bad guy" for fear we will either wrongfully accuse someone, or perhaps not take into account the conditions that made them such dismal and negative individuals.

You won't hear me preach that kind of gospel in The Four W's. Weasels are bad, negative folks—we don't want them around, and Warriors don't make excuses for them. Whiners are nonproductive, and there is nothing wrong with pointing that fact out to them. The Four W's is about being *proactive* to make everything run better.

It is also a simple-to-use business tool that will help you assess situations more accurately, with more confidence, and ultimately aid in making the right decisions. In my career, I have always found that the right path is to "go with your gut," but trusting your instincts isn't always that easy. The Four W's helped me overcome the doubt that often made me hesitate to take the action that in my heart I knew was correct.

HOW MY EXPERIENCE CAN HELP
YOU ACHIEVE YOUR GOALS

As I've mentioned, my philosophies on business and life, and the philosophies of The Four W's, were developed in the field—while running real companies and working with real people in real-life settings. They are derived from my own successes and failures, and my contact with people ranging from successful Warriors to the lowest Weasels. In the course of this book, you will meet some of these real people—in person—and for obvious reasons, some of them will be presented anonymously.

These are not theories formulated by college professors who have never worked outside of academia. My academic credentials end with a degree from a state university. Nor is this one of those personal development books filled with pithy little sayings to memorize in the hope that they alone will make you successful. You make your own success or failure in life, and slogans just aren't enough to make the difference. If you are reading this book in the hope that just owning it will make you more successful, think again.

This book is about assessing yourself, having the fortitude and confidence to make the changes needed to make yourself more successful, and finally, gaining the peace of mind to enjoy what you've earned. And here's an important tip: Warriors are never lazy—it takes work. This book is a tool. Consider the hammer. Simply owning a hammer doesn't mean you will have the finest house on the block, but knowing how to use it and finally putting that talent into action is the first step toward achieving that goal.

Bottom line: The Four W's concept is really just a technique to reaffirm what you already innately understand. You've known Warriors, Workers, Whiners, and Weasels your entire life. Now it's time to deal with the facts, and use what you've always known to your benefit.

• • • • • • • • • • • •

In the next chapter, we will take a look at a few Warriors who set great examples for all of us.

CHAPTER 3

The Ultimate Warriors:
Ten Warriors Who Made
a Big Difference

"It's hard to beat a person who never gives up."
—Babe Ruth

Luckily for all of us, the good guys have always outnumbered the bad in society. It is one thing to be a Warrior and use your Warrior tools to be successful—but a few outstanding souls take their Warrior traits and devote their lives (figuratively and literally) to the common good.

I know most Warriors and Warriors-on-the-cusp who are reading this book are doing so primarily to help achieve their personal goals—which probably don't necessarily involve saving the planet or their fellow man. But I would be remiss if I didn't devote a little space to profiling some of the really incredible Warriors who have lived or are living truly astounding lives.

There are tens of thousands of great Warrior tales, but here are a just a few accounts of these kind of uber Warriors. They range from those who gave their entire lives to their causes, to others who have simply made public service a big part of their lives, or when confronted with the option, simply did the right (albeit difficult) thing. Some are famous, others you have probably never heard of, but all deserve our recognition.

MAXIMILLIAN KOLBE: A WORLD WAR II HERO

Of the many Warrior stories to emerge from the horrors of World War II and the Nazi concentration camps, Maximillian Kolbe's is one of the most heroic. Father Kolbe was a Polish priest imprisoned in Auschwitz in 1941. When one of the men in Kolbe's bunker disappeared and presumably escaped, the Nazis decided to take ten men from the bunker and starve them to death as an example to the others. (Tragically, the missing man was later found drowned in a camp latrine.) When one of the men selected to die cried out in despair that he would never get to see his wife and children again, Father Kolbe stepped forward and asked to take his place. The Nazis complied.

After two weeks of starvation, four of the ten men, including Father Kolbe, were still alive. The Nazis needed their cells for more inmates, so the four were finished off with an injection of carbolic acid.

Father Kolbe was reportedly the last to die, sacrificing his life for a man he barely knew.

AUNG SAN SUU KYI: HUMAN RIGHTS HERO

Like the South African leader Nelson Mandela before her, Burmese freedom fighter Aung San Suu Kyi[1] has come to be seen internationally as a symbol of heroic and peaceful resistance in the face of oppression. Burma has one of the worst human rights records of any nation in the world, and despite her frequent arrests and detainment, Suu Kyi continues to fight the battle for freedom for her native land, leading Burma's main pro-democracy party, The National League for Democracy.

And this is a life Suu Kyi has chosen, not one that was thrust upon her. The daughter of the late Burmese nationalist leader General Aung San, she initially migrated to India and then to Britain where she received her education and met her husband, an Oxford University academic. Suu Kyi certainly could have remained in Britain and lived a wonderful and peaceful

---

1. BBC News Special Report, August 9, 1998.

life, but she returned to Burma in 1988 to lead the call for democracy and fight the brutal government repression.

This led to her house arrest for six years (in fact, she is still under certain government restrictions). In 1991, while still under house arrest, she was awarded the Nobel Peace Prize, and today as she continues her activism, the government is still restricting her right to move and speak.

JAMES REEB: CIVIL RIGHTS HERO

Born into poverty in a small Pennsylvania town, James Reeb[2] went on to become one of the heroes of the civil rights movement in the 1960s. After serving in WWII, Reeb became a minister with the Unitarian Church, settling in Washington DC. After five years there, he felt his calling was to minister to people even more in need, and he relocated to the poor section of Roxbury in Boston to assist the inner city poor.

In 1965, Reeb was working to get the city of Boston to revamp its housing and safety codes to aid the poor residents of his neighborhood, when he watched on the news as "Bloody Sunday" unfolded. On March 7, 1965, Alabama state troopers used billy clubs, bullwhips, and tear gas to break up a peaceful civil rights march from Selma to the capital in Birmingham.

The next day, when Martin Luther King appealed to clergy from around the world to join him for a minister's march, Reeb answered the call, arriving in Alabama on March 9th. After spending the day in peaceful protests with other ministers, Reeb and two other ministers were attacked while returning to their hotel after dinner. Three white men shouting racial epithets savagely beat them, clubbing Reeb in the head. He died from his injuries two days later.

Reeb's death became a focal point for the movement and helped progress it. Congress expressed outrage and moved for government intervention. Deeply moved by the death of "that good man," President Lyndon B. Johnson immediately began drafting the voting rights bill that would help move forward the civil rights movement. More than thirty thousand people attended Reeb's memorial service the following Saturday in Boston.

---

2. Duncan Howlett, *No Greater Love: The James Reeb Story* (Harper and Row, 1966).

ALEXANDRA SCOTT: LITTLE GIRL WITH A BIG AGENDA—RAISING MONEY FOR CANCER RESEARCH

Alexandra Scott proves that age is no barrier to becoming a Warrior. Before she died of cancer at the age of eight, she had raised more than $1.5 million for cancer research.

Diagnosed with neuroblatoma—an aggressive form of childhood cancer—during her first year, Alex went on to make the most of her short life. She began by setting up a lemonade stand in front of her house to raise money for cancer research—raising $2,000 her first year. After appearing on *Today* and *The Oprah Winfrey Show*, lemonade fund-raisers were set up in all fifty states, with Alex becoming the spokesperson for the cause, despite her waning health.

And the cause that Alex championed continues today, with a goal this year of raising more than $5 million.

HARRY CHAPIN: FIGHTING TO REDUCE WORLD HUNGER

Many 1970s music fans will remember folksinger Harry Chapin for hits like "Taxi" and "Cats in the Cradle." During a tremendous career cut short by his death in an auto accident, Chapin released ten albums and toured throughout the world.

But shortly after releasing his first hit album, Chapin decided to use his musical gift and fame to combat world hunger. In 1974, he founded WHY (World Hunger Year), an organization that still exists almost twenty years after his death. He set out to educate people on the issues of world hunger and to raise money to help solve the problem.

Throughout the remainder of his career, Chapin donated much of the proceeds from his tours and record and merchandise sales to this and other charities aimed at fighting hunger. He helped found and fund other hunger charities, including Hungerthon and Long Island Cares.

In 1986, Chapin was posthumously awarded a Congressional Gold Medal for his tremendous work. A memorial fund started at his death to continue his work has raised more than $5 million for a variety of social causes that were close to his heart.

WANGARI MAATHAI: FIGHTING POVERTY AND ENVIRONMENTAL PROBLEMS

The first black African woman ever to be awarded a Nobel Prize, Wangari Maathai started the Green Belt Movement in Kenya in 1977. Maathai launched the organization in a joint effort to protect the environment and assist African women. A corrupt government was allowing rapid deforestation around many Kenyan villages. As Maathai began to organize to combat the practice, she realized that destroying forests was not only an environmental disaster; it was a human one as well. There was no firewood for the poor villages that depended on wood for fuel for cooking and hygiene.

Maathai tackled both problems, beginning a protracted battle against the corrupt government to save the forests and help the desperately poor women and their children. Over the years, she has been beaten, arrested, and frequently detained for her efforts—but she has stayed true to her cause, culminating in 1997, when she was elected to Parliament.

SOMPOP JANKTRAKA: FIGHTING THE ASIAN SEX SLAVE TRADE

Named "One of 25 Asian Heroes" by *Time* magazine in 2002, Sompop Janktraka has devoted his life to saving Thai children from the horrors of sex slavery. In many poor Thai villages, young girls have unfortunately become a commodity, sold to human traffickers to work as prostitutes. Brothel owners comb the poor villages, looking for destitute families that will sell a child just so the rest of the family can survive. Rampant disease, including a horrible AIDS epidemic, has made this a death sentence for many Thai children.

Janktraka helped found and runs DEPDC, a school and home to help keep children safe from being trafficked into the sex industry. So far, DEPDC has saved more than one thousand children.

MIJA HOWLETT: HELPING DRUG ADDICTS

Much closer to home, Mija Howlett[3] is also doing her best to save lives. The former drug addict is now an AIDS counselor in Missoula, Montana—

---

3. *Montana Kaimin*, April 25, 2005.

spending her days and nights counseling and treating AIDS victims, and those at risk to become victims. As a $10-an-hour worker for The AIDS Council and Curry Health Center, she administers free counseling and testing to those who might be infected with AIDS and hepatitis C.

But Howlett's work extends far beyond the clinic. When she leaves the clinic, she cruises parks where high-risk individuals might be hanging out, handing out condoms and clean needles in hopes of preventing transmission of the diseases and educating those with questions. Howlett knows that the key to keeping the infections in check is to stop high-risk behavior, and to identify the infected as soon as possible to cut back on more transmissions.

At night, she counsels the afflicted and potentially afflicted in their home territories, going to bars to discuss AIDS prevention and treatment. On an average night, she will convince several high-risk individuals to get tested right away, and they return to the clinic with her to administer late night tests. Other times, she is awakened in the middle of the night by drug abusers who need clean needles to minimize their risk of infection, and she drags herself out of bed at 4 A.M. to make the deliveries. Although she always attempts to get the abusers to kick their habits, she knows that at least she can potentially stop them from becoming infected—and infecting others—with a potential fatal disease.

Howlett's personal story of redemption to emerge a Warrior is particularly powerful. Growing up in Sacramento, she began using drugs early. At age thirteen, while tripping on acid, she was at a house where several others were using heroin. When she rejected their attempts to get her to try the drug, they bound her to a coffee table, injected her with heroin, and raped her. For the next six years, she fought drug addiction, finally beating it when she moved to Montana at age nineteen. Now she devotes her life to helping and saving others who are fighting the battle she was able to win.

JIM BARKSDALE: PROMOTING LITERACY IN POOR NEIGHBORHOODS

Jim Barksdale certainly achieved the typical Warrior's dream of success. The former Netscape CEO was at the forefront of the Internet boom, and he made a fortune in the process.

But the Mississippi native was willing to give back, donating $100 million to form the Barksdale Reading Institute, a nonprofit foundation dedicated to promoting literacy among preschoolers through third graders in poor neighborhoods. The institute is now working with seventy-one schools, providing books, teachers, and training for children who would have no other options.

STEVE WRIGHT: GIVING SOMETHING BACK

Of course, not all of us are willing or in a position to dedicate our entire professional lives, or $100 million, to the common good. But it's encouraging to see that socially minded Warriors come in every shape and size. Although we have been especially barraged over the last few years by greedy CEOs and con men, Steve Wright[4] stands out as a model for corporate executives.

While serving as the head of the Bonneville Power Administration three years ago, he returned a $7,500 bonus that he was entitled to because he "didn't feel right about taking a bonus when his agency was losing money." Although the bonus represented 5 percent of his salary, Wright said he just couldn't accept it under the circumstances. Imagine if more corporate CEOs adopted this position!

· · · · · · · · · · · ·

For more Warrior stories, or to submit a story about your favorite Warrior, go to www.warriorsandweasels.com. In the next chapter, we will detail the core tenet of being a Warrior or a Worker: **Rights = Responsibility.**

---

4. AP, July 4, 2002.

CHAPTER 4

Rights = Responsibility: Recognize That You're Not *Entitled* to Success

---

"The Constitution only gives people the right to pursue happiness.
You have to catch it yourself."
—Ben Franklin

One of the consistent themes of The Four W's is **RIGHTS = RE-SPONSIBILITY**.[1] As I will state many times and in many ways during the course of this book, the idea that society owes us anything but an equal playing field, and the opportunity and freedom to prove ourselves and control our own destinies is a dangerous mind-set. Instead, we actually have an obligation to society: to guide it, form it, and hopefully leave it better for generations to come. It is each of our individual responsibilities to stand up for and fight for our rights, be they in the workplace, in our governmental structure, or even in our personal lives.

---

1. As much as I would like to take responsibility for the phrase RIGHTS = RESPONSIBILITY, I must credit Jim Russell for the concept.

SUCCESS IS NOT A BIRTHRIGHT

The last few American generations have lived in historically privileged times. American military, social, and economic dominance has spoiled us a bit. It is easy to believe that just because we are here in this place and time, we were somehow destined for success. But success is not a birthright, and as history has consistently demonstrated, every great society has ultimately stumbled. America was not "chosen" by divine intervention to lead the world, and we can quickly go the way of the Roman and British empires if we don't constantly address our responsibilities. We are in this position because of the talents and sacrifices of the generations that preceded us, and we have an obligation to build upon the legacy they have left us.

We have built perhaps the greatest social system in the history of the world to date, based on the concept that "all men (and women) are created equal," and as a culture based on immigration, we take pride in the idea that anyone from any background can achieve success in the U.S. if they put forward the effort. In fact, to a great extent, our society was built on the *rejection* of the idea of entitlement. Instead, we have a system that rewards innovation and hard work for anyone willing to expend the effort. This philosophy has consistently driven us to perform above those societies that put more restrictions on the individual and that fail to provide the necessary incentives for advancement.

But with these rights come responsibility, and unfortunately, many people now expect to enjoy these rights without taking the responsibility to maintain the privilege. And accepting responsibility and all that it entails can be the most freeing experience possible, as ultimately depending on yourself is the key to independence.

ACCEPT RESPONSIBILITY FOR YOUR COMMUNITY

Do you want to maintain the right to vote in free elections? Then accept the responsibility to actually research candidates and issues, take an informed stand, and actually go to the trouble to vote. Those who proudly declare: "I don't vote; I'm not interested in politics," or "I don't vote because it doesn't mean anything" are fools and a threat to the concept of free elections. Perhaps the only bigger threat is the active voters who do not take the responsibility to properly educate themselves on the issues, and choose their leaders and government mandate based on rumor and hype.

Unfortunately, the spread of mass media and the Internet has actually increased our responsibilities as citizens. We are now besieged with thousands of messages a day through the myriad of television channels, radio stations, and online communications that surround us. The issues that confront all of us are more complex, and our vision for our government must now be global, whether we like it or not. The responsibility falls to each of us to sift through this "mountain of messages" to determine the truth.

Do you want the right to free speech? Then accept the responsibility to publicly oppose those who would take that right away from you for any reason. Do the research to completely understand issues. Sometimes, protecting our most sacred rights might involve protecting those we don't agree with to maintain the freedoms essential to all of us. Freedom is not achieved by taking away freedoms. Don't fall prey to fears that allow others to take away your rights, as fear is always temporary, but freedom has to be a constant for future generations.

Do you want the right to safe streets, affordable healthcare, good schools, and a clean environment? Then accept the responsibility to pay for your fair share via taxes; make occasional sacrifices to achieve long-term goals; perhaps donate some of your time and effort toward your favorite cause. If there is crime in your neighborhood, get proactive and work with the authorities and your other neighbors to eliminate it. Confront the creeps! Accept the responsibility that a secure future involves more than your personal success: that, in fact, prosperity for everyone who can possibly achieve it will make your life better. Accept the responsibility to help monitor the performance of our elected officials to make sure they are achieving the goals the community has set for them.

And the concept of **RIGHTS = RESPONSIBILITY** extends far beyond the political and social big picture. Warriors embrace the concept because they know it puts them at a decisive advantage over those who shun responsibility.

So here's what you can do.

ACCEPT RESPONSIBILITY FOR YOUR FAMILY

Do you want the right to have a terrific family with great happy kids who grow up to be wonderful adults (and hopefully provide you some pleasure in your old age)? Then accept the responsibility to be a role model, by setting a positive example, disciplining when necessary, and making the necessary sacrifices the family requires. Parents aren't supposed to be their kids "buddies"—they have an obligation to set the proper example and take tough disciplinary action when required. Don't let your kids rule the house and develop bad habits that will haunt them throughout their lives. Insert yourself into their lives as more than a spectator. Take the time to train them to be good citizens, and they will be good to you.

ACCEPT RESPONSIBILITY FOR A BETTER WORKPLACE

Do you want the right to be more successful at work? Then accept the responsibility to make your company more efficient, more profitable, and a better place to be. Just showing up on time is not the same as taking responsibility. No matter how large the organization you work for, you play an important part in the health and profitability (or lack of profitability) of the company. I spend tens of thousands of dollars per year flying across the country. I frequently base the decision of which airline to fly on how well I am treated by the flight attendants and gate agents, as I know many other businesspeople do. Our primary point of contact are the people at the counter and the people seating us and serving us drinks. I can think of dozens of other similar situations in which the employees who in many ways control the destiny of the company are certainly not the obvious decision makers, and it is integral that they understand their important role. Complaining to your friends about how you hate your job is not the same as constructively working with management to improve your workplace. Accept the responsibility to admit you are part of the structure, not just a mindless cog in the machine, and do your best to constantly improve your performance and work conditions, and assist those of the same mind-set.

ACCEPT RESPONSIBILITY FOR A HAPPIER, HEALTHIER LIFE

Do you want the right to live a long, happy, and healthy life? Then accept the responsibility to treat your body with sufficient care. Eat a reasonable diet and keep your weight within an acceptable range. Take the time to get regular exercise. Find a relaxing hobby that helps you recharge. Keep yourself mentally challenged. Read, stay informed about current events, and endeavor to continue learning on a daily basis. Don't abuse your system with excessive tobacco, alcohol, and drugs, or let yourself become obese, and then expect the medical system to keep you at the same peak levels as those who took the responsibility to care for themselves. Your addictions and weaknesses are your problem. Deal with them and don't expect society to bail you out.

And take time to enjoy the result of your hard work. Go on vacation and find a few regular endeavors that you really enjoy. Don't adhere to such stringent standards in your life that you let the good things pass you by.

ACCEPT RESPONSIBILITY FOR YOUR FINANCES

Do you want the right to be financially stable and successful, and enjoy the perks that financial security affords? Then accept the responsibility to work to achieve this, and avoid the addictions and pitfalls that can set you back. Live within a reasonable budget, put away enough for contingencies, and plan for your retirement. Exercise some self-control over your purchases. Personal debt should be restricted to your home and perhaps an auto, not extended to credit cards that allow you to finance consumptive items such as clothes and big screen televisions. Excessive debt is a form of slavery, limiting options and sometimes forcing people to make terrible choices and take the path of the Whiner or Weasel.

If you can't pay for it, save up until you can afford it; don't pay credit card companies huge windfalls so you can live above your means. Always make the assumption that *you*—not the government or someone else—will have to take care of yourself in your old age. The concept sounds simple, but too many people incorrectly assume someone else has the responsibility to make sure their lives turn out well.

WARRIORS AND WORKERS ACCEPT THEIR RESPONSIBILITIES

Whiners and Weasels shun responsibility, but they insist on the rights. In contrast, Warriors and Workers understand you earn what you achieve, and one of the most precious rights we possess is the individual's opportunity to confidently pursue his or her dream and enjoy the freedom of self-reliance.

* * * * * * * * * * * *

In the next section, we delve deeper into the Warrior's world, and detail some of the attributes it requires to take control of your own life.

PART TWO

Are You A Warrior?
(And If Not, How to Become One)

WARRIORS

CHAPTER 5

Profile of a Warrior: ("The Duke" Taught You Everything You Need to Know)

"If you are unsure of how to pronounce a word,
say it more loudly."
—E.B. White

I grew up watching and loving John Wayne movies. Like most movie action heroes, the Duke had a formula to his success. In his films, he was always the loner, a little uncomfortable around people, but undyingly faithful to his friends (even weird friends like screeching, gimpy Walter Brennan, whining Glenn Campbell, or a constantly inebriated Dean Martin). He was a family man when he had a family, even though he would sometimes leave them for long periods of time (presumably because he was off fighting evil or pursuing revenge against one-eyed murderers).

The Duke had a simple code of right and wrong that he never violated. He had disdain for authority when authority became arrogant, bureaucratic, or sinister. He trusted his instincts. He was full of faults, ranging from drunkenness to surliness, to the fact that he wore the same clothes in more than seventy films. He never lied or cheated people who didn't deserve it, and he was absolutely fearless when it came to Weasels. He insulted them, shot them, threatened them, chased them, and smacked them around—and always with a pithy remark before he took his revenge. He was the consummate Warrior—and a Weasel-destroying force to be reckoned with.

Okay, I've heard the anti-Duke stories, but I'm not here to debate the merits of the real-life John/Marion Wayne versus the cinema persona. The fact is that the movie Duke is one of the best twentieth century representations of "The Warrior."

UNDERSTANDING THE WARRIOR MENTALITY

Although many of you reading this book are probably seeking the business and financial success that frequently comes with being a Warrior, the Warrior mentality is not necessarily centered on just growing rich and/or powerful. Rather, the traits that a Warrior possesses just happen to be the traits that tend to make one more successful in life and in business. That being said, Warriors also tend to gravitate toward less financially lucrative professions just because it suits their personalities. Warriors are competitive and action-oriented, and accordingly, they naturally seek out professions that allow them to make a difference through their own initiative. Warriors luxuriate in the almost-constant buzz that a feeling of self-confidence and determination provides, and they are constantly establishing new and more difficult goals to achieve.

In addition to business, it's easy to find Warriors in law enforcement, the armed forces, political and social activism, firefighting and other emergency services, certain areas of healthcare, professional sports, education, and even politics and the law (although as one might suspect, the latter of these arenas is also a hotbed for Weasels). Let's look at Warriors in a few characteristic lines of work in more detail.

WARRIORS IN THE MILITARY

Warriors in the military quickly work their way up to high ranks or into the more challenging branches of the service: Navy Seals, Green Berets, Paratroopers, and the other action-oriented areas. Although they accept and understand the need for military structure, in their souls, they find the constraints and bureaucracy difficult to tolerate. They need to command and make a difference, or be left to their own devices to effect change. Sometimes this leads to successful but turbulent careers. Generals George S. Patton and George Armstrong Custer were good examples of Warriors who had a love/hate relationship with the military structure (hence, both reached an early plateau as far as the military structure was concerned, and they were subsequently demoted as their careers progressed). Most soldiers are actually workers, so the Warriors either quickly distinguish themselves as officers and/or heroes, or they leave the service to find more appropriate professions that don't place limitations on their personalities.

WARRIORS IN THE HELPING/HEALING PROFESSIONS

Warriors entering the medical field gravitate toward being paramedics, emergency room doctors and nurses, research scientists attacking diseases, surgeons, and other proactive areas within the profession. They love the fact that they can make a dramatic difference via their actions, and they crave the importance of their duties. Every major medical disaster around the world tends to draw these kinds of Warriors, and they make the often difficult and dangerous trek to help those in need. There are also many health and child care activist/Warriors who devote their lives to helping those who can't help themselves.

WARRIORS IN THE LEGAL FIELD

Warriors in the legal field are drawn to litigation and negotiation. Although the majority of the population tends to shun confrontation, or be inept at handling it, Warriors embrace a spirited disagreement and competition. They have the self-confidence and skill set to win—hence, the natural draw toward confrontation.

Although one might assume that the legal field in general would be full of Warriors; in truth, most legal work is mundane, and it tends to draw high-level workers, and, of course, the layer of Weasels who are attracted to the image of potentially easy money and the opportunity to take advantage of people while in some strange way boosting their egos. The public image of the legal profession is a dichotomy between the Warriors we admire (Perry Mason, Matlock, and the cavalcade of John Grisham legal heroes), and the classic ambulance-chasing Weasel-lawyers we disdain.

The greatest legal Warriors fight the great and necessary fight to maintain everyone else's rights, and do constant battle with the Weasels who would seek to take those rights away.

WARRIORS IN SPORTS

As one would suspect, professional sports—both at the player and coach's level—is primarily a profession of Warriors. As I write this, Lance Armstrong certainly comes to mind as one of the greatest Warriors in the history of sports. It is almost impossible to compete professionally without some Warrior attributes, and in its purest form, competitive athletics, when combined with the gentlemanly aspects of the game, is the essence of the Warrior mentality. Unfortunately, the infusion of huge money and corporate sponsorships into the field is having a negative impact. Impressionable young player/Warriors are being seduced by the Weasels who control much of the big money surrounding sports, changing the essence of the games and often converting the player to Weasel-status. Unfortunately, it is just as common to see today's sports heroes sitting in front of a congressional hearing detailing their use of designer drugs as playing on the field. Sportsmanship is being replaced by money-raising antics, which runs counter to the soul of the Warrior.

WARRIORS IN OTHER FIELDS

Although certain professions have a much stronger and more natural draw, you will potentially find Warriors in any field. Most of us have had charismatic teachers that embodied the Warrior mentality, dedicated to their vision of more enlightened generations to come. I have had the pleasure of meeting many environmental and social activists that live by a strict Warrior's code. Many Warriors are drawn to arts and entertainment.

WARRIOR POLITICIANS

Regardless of how you feel about their politics, it's impossible to classify people like Ralph Nader, Pat Buchanan, Bill and Hillary Clinton, Robert Kennedy, Jerry Brown, John McCain, Martin Luther King Jr., and the many other political and social activists as anything but Warriors (though many may argue that some are "Warriors with strong Weasel tendencies"). Although they are certainly driven by their egos, they are motivated by what they regard as positive societal ideals, and they spend their lives fighting to make them a reality. Their quests require that they bare their souls to the public and allow their personal lives to become targets for those who disagree with them.

Equally distracting is the fact that politics (like many other egocentric professions) often blurs the lines and confuses the Warrior. To be a Warrior, you need to have a sense of purpose and self-confidence (often frequently associated with arrogance) to see your vision to fruition. When he was in his early twenties, Bill Clinton announced to his friends with full conviction that someday he would be the president of the United States, an audacious claim at the time for a young man with poor roots from Arkansas. This necessary self-confidence/arrogance is often perceived as self-serving—and sometimes does threaten to convert Warriors to Weasels.

"DARK WARRIORS"

Unfortunately, the Warrior spirit can also sometimes be infected with mental illness or fanaticism, or it can just be devoid of a soul; hence, history is full of Warriors-gone-bad. I call them Dark Warriors. They have the drive and aggression of a Warrior, but they live and breathe like the worst possible Weasel. Since I first wrote this chapter, I had to rewrite this section to include one of the worst Dark Warriors our nation has ever had to confront: Osama bin Laden. He joins a long list of Dark Warriors— men like Slobodan Milosevic, Moammar Gadhafi, Adolf Hitler, Joseph Stalin, and many others who took their passion and drive the wrong way. They are much more powerful than Weasels could ever hope to be. Power simply for the sake of power is a Weasel-aphrodisiac, and many budding Warriors have been converted to the dark side by the lure of it.

The image of the Dark Warrior has even been interwoven throughout our culture. We are fascinated by the concept of a talented and charismatic individual who, for whatever reason, chooses to use his or her talents to do bad. Religion is filled with many representations of the Dark Warrior, beginning with Lucifer and his gang who were ejected from heaven. Darth Vadar is the fictional poster-boy for the Dark Warrior— the brilliant Warrior gone bad to ravage the universe.

We sometimes even cheer on these Dark Warriors. Consider the fact that one of the most popular and celebrated characters currently on television, Tony Soprano, makes his living killing people and committing crimes. The media's tendency to sometimes glorify Dark Warriors is an increasing problem in society. Fifty years ago, movie screens were filled with stories featuring "tough guy" thugs like Edgar G. Robinson, but today's kids often worship "Gangster Rappers" who frequently really do live life on and off the screen immersed in crime.

OTHER NEGATIVE ASPECTS OF WARRIORS

Warriors seldom choose to be Warriors. Rather, it is an inbred attitude that sometimes even causes pain. Many Warriors are constantly walking that fine line between brilliance and a vision gone amok. They become too driven—too concerned about the minutia that leads to the achievement of their goals. They are frequently obtuse about others, assuming that everyone shares their Warrior attributes, which often gives them unrealistic expectations about their employees, coworkers, and loved ones. That is why it is crucial for the successful Warrior to be aware of the other "three W's," so they can foster talent among budding Warriors and set realistic expectations for the Workers in their world.

A Warrior's passion sometimes drives him or her a little too far; they end up hurting those they care about, which leads the Warrior into a private depression. Because Warriors hate to whine, they have difficulty expressing this feeling, which tends to exacerbate the situation. Unfortunately, this can sometimes take a Warrior down the Hemingway path, when passion and drive and brilliance succumb to depression. By their very nature, Warriors are emotional souls, though their emotions may take a different form than most people's. The key for the Warrior is channeling this emotion and drive to maintain happiness, while not getting bogged down in the emotional wake that the Warrior's passion creates.

HOW TO BE A SUCCESSFUL WARRIOR

So the key to being a successful Warrior is keeping all the positive attributes and drive in check—succeeding without causing unnecessary damage—and achieving an end result of satisfaction for a job well done. The healthy, productive Warrior achieves this through judicious use of all the tools at his or her disposal, which I like to call the Warrior's Toolbox—which leads us to the next chapter.

The Warrior's Toolbox: Ten Tools Every Warrior Should Possess

"Nothing succeeds like reputation."
— John Huston

Successful Warriors—and those who aspire to be a Warrior—possess a mental toolbox, a collection of personality attributes, talents, and rules-to-live-by that they call on constantly. These tools, when properly fostered, maintained, and utilized, make success achievable. And when used improperly, they can quickly take the Warrior or Warrior wannabe down the wrong path—to failure. There is often a fine line between being a Warrior and being an arrogant bully or blowhard (a line I unfortunately have crossed a few times), so Warriors have to constantly be on guard, making sure they properly utilize their talents and gifts.

Of course, every Warrior personalizes his or her toolbox, and perhaps adds more tools that are particularly appropriate for his or her needs, but the following are tools that most Warriors possess in some form. If you are a Worker on the verge of becoming a Warrior, or a Whiner or Weasel cognizant of your situation and anxious to change your life, this chapter is a good opportunity to take an inventory of your own tools to determine what needs to be added to your toolbox. Even if you don't aspire to be a Warrior, utilizing a few of these tools will be beneficial in many areas of your life.

And as any good craftsman will tell you, owning the right tools is only part of the battle; knowing how to use them is even more important. Many "Warriors-on-the-cusp" are simply misusing the tools they already possess, and this chapter will help you hone your skills. Others may own the tools, but they will never possess the skill to properly utilize them, which leads to all kind of other problems. Figure 6-1 lists the ten tools that every Warrior should possess; once you've seen the quick overview, let's open the toolbox.

Figure 6-1: Ten Tools Every Warrior Should Possess

1. The Integrity Tool
2. The "I'll Make It Happen" Tool
3. The Self-responsibility Tool
4. The Intuition Tool
5. A Personal Brand
6. The Relationship Tool
7. The "Talk Is Cheap" Tool
8. The Trust Tool
9. The Guidepost and Reward Tool
10. The Compassion Tool

#1: THE INTEGRITY TOOL

Like it or not, you can always depend on Warriors to tell you how they feel—and to do what they say they will do. This is the single most important tool the Warrior (or a good Worker) possesses. Without it, the rest of the toolbox is virtually worthless. In fact, you should envision integrity as a key component to all your tools—like the handle, the battery, or the power cord that makes your tools function. Successful Warriors protect their integrity above all else, as they know it is the primary currency they trade with. It is the core of their "personal brand" and key to their relationships, other important tools that I will discuss later in this chapter.

Your Word Is Your Bond. If your coworkers, employees, clients, suppliers, family, or others you come in contact with have valid reason to doubt your word, it negates all the other good work you do, and it puts you at a constant disadvantage, from multiple respects. The basis of great long-term business and family relationships is trusting that all parties will stand by their word and do what they promise. Bottom line: always endeavor to do what you say you are going to do. Make your word your bond, and take pride in the fact that you can be trusted. Insist that those you deal with adopt the same philosophy, and make it an understood requirement to do business with you.

But don't mistake the Warrior's integrity for some high-mindedness that puts him or her on a higher moral or intellectual plain than non-Warriors. As wonderful as this sounds in theory, Warriors come from every walk of life, and they have goals, viewpoints, and philosophies as varied as the general population. I am not here to tell you that simply being a Warrior makes you a superior individual to others. Although they go into many wonderful endeavors that benefit the masses, Warriors also run tobacco companies, adult film studios, shady law practices, brothels, and other less-than-reputable enterprises. But Warriors are consistent and dependable in their approach, which is an appealing attribute to others.

The integrity tool, as we are discussing it here, simply relates to the ability to "do what you say you are going to do," which is unfortunately not what all of us would consider the "right" thing to do. I do advocate that Warriors report to a higher calling and attempt to utilize their talents for positive endeavors, but this book is not about any one social or moral philosophy.

Don't Make Promises You Can't Keep. Making your word your bond has many implications, not just about integrity, but also about assessing what can and can't be accomplished. Warriors often have "eyes bigger than their plates," which gives them a tendency to overpromise, despite their good intentions. Promising anything "just to get the deal" when you know you can't deliver is a Weasel technique, and a shortsighted way to operate.

For example, over the last couple of years, I started using a contractor to do some remodeling around my house. He has always provided good craftsmanship, for what I believe was a fair price, though the truth is I liked him so much that I eventually gave up getting alternate bids. This saved us both time and angst, and I figured that even if he was slightly higher in price, I was willing to pay more for consistent quality and dependability. However, he completed the last two projects months past his estimated delivery date. It turns out he had booked another major project after accepting my projects, but instead of explaining the situation to me so we could come to an agreement, he just continued to make promises that he couldn't deliver on. He certainly didn't do it maliciously, but he should have either delivered on the date promised, or had an honest discussion with me so we could negotiate a fair compromise. But because he didn't, he has destroyed my trust in him, and now as I look at a major project for next year, I have decided I will not even take a bid from him.

Although Warriors might have the best intentions, if they consistently overpromise for even the best of reasons and fail to deliver, or fail to deliver on a timely basis, they soon appear to have lost their integrity to the rest of the world—and they lose their Warrior status. It's essential to have reasonable expectations before promising—and to tailor your promises to reality. It is far better in the long run to make realistic promises that can be accomplished, than to gain a reputation for never living up to your word.

Integrity is also not only a function of simply doing what you say you are going to do, but also telling the hard truths. I've seen many Warriors-on-the-cusp fail to make the grade because they can't make the difficult phone call or visit to give someone bad news. Hence, they live as *conflict avoiders*, a serious condition I will frequently reference throughout the book.

In the example above, the way for my contractor to redeem himself was to tell the hard truth, and let me know that he could not finish the job as promised. Although I would have been temporarily upset, I would have respected his honesty, and if he had completed the job by the new date he promised, he would have at least maintained his standing in my eyes.

Certainly there would have been a variety of acceptable compromises that would have left us both feeling good about the deal.

As you will see later in the book, sometimes being a Warrior involves "going out on a limb" and making promises that you know will be difficult to keep, but you intend to fulfill at any cost. "Intent with a gung-ho expectation to deliver" is a lot different than "taking the order and hoping somehow it all comes together." Warriors fully expect to deliver.

Don't Be a Coward: Deal with Difficult Situations. For several years, I had an employee who was showing tremendous Warrior potential, and I spent a lot of time working with him to progress through the organization. He was full of new ideas, his work was typically good, and he put in a tremendous amount of effort and hours without complaining. In almost every way, he was a perfect employee.

The problem was he was a conflict avoider—with clients and with me. No matter what, he just could not face conflicts, which meant I or someone else in the organization had to perform the "tough jobs" for him.

To compound the problem, when I would confront him about his conflict avoidance, he did everything in his power to avoid a conflict with me over the issue, quickly trying to pass over and ignore the problem. Of course, this greatly reduced his value to the organization, and he quickly topped out in his career. As I got to know him better personally, I discovered that this conflict avoidance had run rampant throughout his life. He had been in a miserable marriage, but he didn't want to confront the hard choices involved in making a change. So, he just endured constant unhappiness. The sad fact was that if he had addressed his conflict avoidance with a few key people in his life and gotten the difficult job over with, he could have eliminated most of the angst he felt on a daily basis.

I find that many conflict avoiders don't even realize they have a problem, as they tend to lie to themselves about the situation. Conflict avoiders don't realize that they are often the only ones who fear conflict in a situation and that confrontation is often healthy in organizations and families. People ultimately lose respect for conflict avoiders, which leads to an entirely new set of problems.

I have had other employees who, as a result of their conflict avoidance, eventually denigrate from good Workers to Whiners. They are unhappy with aspects of their job or their compensation, but instead of going to their supervisors to discuss their situations, they hold it all inside, eventually taking their complaints to coworkers, friends, family members, or others who have no power to improve the situation. Small complaints with no resolution often grow exponentially, and soon these employees hate everything about their jobs and are quick to point it out to anyone who will listen (with the exception of anyone who could actually improve their plight). Sadly, the people who could change the work environment are often totally unaware that the employee is unhappy.

Warriors also realize that for them to do a good job in their position, they have to feel valuable, respected, and properly compensated. Therefore, if they have a problem at work, they are the first to candidly and calmly discuss it with their supervisors, as it is to the benefit of all involved to address the issue and move on to more productive work. If they feel they deserve a promotion or raise, they go to their boss and express their case—properly documented to achieve their goal. They don't let it fester and impact their work.

Conflict avoidance is also common in families, as it is a trait that can be taught and passed down. For example, a good friend of mine comes from a large family that suffers from one of the most serious mass conflict avoidance problems I have ever seen. The parents and the siblings are totally incapable of telling each other how they really feel when there is any form of disagreement, so instead, they express their negative opinions to everyone except those involved, resulting in a family situation that now seems to thrive on gossip and whining. This mass conflict avoidance taints what otherwise could be a great family relationship.

Often, the tendency to avoid conflicts becomes the biggest factor that keeps people from attaining Warrior status. Warriors' ability to tackle tough situations without delay gives them an enormous advantage over people who waste time lamenting the situation and delaying the dreaded duty. Warriors may not like firing people, calling clients to collect money, or letting them know a problem or mistake has occurred, but they get it over with for the good of the organization, as opposed to the well-meaning conflict avoiders who hold the organization back because they don't want to be the bearer of bad tidings. Although it may be painful to give loved ones, clients, coworkers, and vendors bad news, the few minutes or few days of discomfort that follows will pay huge dividends in the long term, because the bearer of bad news has much more integrity than a conflict avoider.

And the fact that conflict avoidance is such a huge problem presents enormous opportunity to the Warrior. When I look at my own staff, my organization is always lacking those who will tackle the tough problems effectively; those who rise through the ranks quickly are willing to confront conflict. Problem solvers are a rare commodity and, accordingly, command a high price and status in the workplace.

The Lack of Integrity Has Become a Societal Problem. Conflict avoidance often deteriorates into a more serious problem—lack of integrity. The fact that integrity is no longer taught and emphasized in most people's lives from birth (as it once was) has necessitated a huge, expensive, and unfortunate societal infrastructure. Think of all the steps we now must take in an attempt to ensure that those around us deal with us with integrity! Almost every step in business now has to be supervised and documented by expensive legal teams that seek to close every possible loophole that would allow someone to violate their word. Our natural assumption is that those we deal with will not possess integrity.

For example, we pay huge sums for legal contracts, insurance, and other safeguards to protect us, built on the sad reality that most people and companies we come in contact with will be ethically challenged if they see an opportunity to exploit. We have a massive and growing myriad of laws designed and executed by a huge infrastructure primarily designed to force people to be honest, and to protect us when they're not.

Integrity Separates the Warriors from Everyone Else. It's certainly a shame that all the energy expended on dealing with the reality that many people have no integrity couldn't be rechanneled into building it as a key personality trait that should be taught to every child from birth. However, Whiners and Weasels discard integrity for a potential shortcut to success on the back of someone else, so ultimately, integrity often becomes the key point of differentiation among Warriors, Weasels, and Whiners: Weasels throw integrity out the window, whenever sacrificing it offers a benefit. Whiners make excuses when they have an integrity lapse, and so, they never learn from the experience.

But the Warrior sees this all as opportunity arising out of societal dysfunction, a clear chance to rise above the crowd. It's crucial that, above all else, the Warrior be able to state with honesty and confidence that "I always do what I say I will do." Possessing integrity when others don't puts one at a decisive advantage for the long term; in my experience, those without integrity generally have short life spans in their positions. They pretend to be Warriors, often getting the great job, but pretending only gets them so far. Possessing credibility and making it a lynchpin of your personal brand draws the attention and confidence of others; without it, you are eventually "discovered."

The Benefits of Integrity. And here's one of the best features of living a life of integrity as a Warrior. Becoming a Warrior is, in a certain sense, like joining an unofficial and secret club, and the potential success of being a Warrior aside, this Warrior club has certain wonderful benefits. Perhaps the biggest one is that real Warriors innately recognize other Warriors, often based on the tenet of integrity. Warriors trust other Warriors, because they know that even without all the safeguards that their lawyers, middlemen, and insurance agents would put into place for them, the right thing will still be done.

This smooths out what can otherwise be a difficult process. Deals often proceed more quickly as Warriors come to verbal agreement and begin a mutually beneficial relationship. Less time and money is spent on protection, and more on production, which is more profitable and fulfilling for all involved. Warriors thrive on relationships (as detailed later in this chapter), and they realize that great relationships are formed with integrity from both sides. The often-discussed and frequently criticized "old boys' club" is often really a Warriors' club—informal groups that have formed relationships based on the fact that, as Warriors, they know they will collectively get the job done.

Integrity Requires Strength. Integrity is an extremely difficult tool to maintain. We are all constantly challenged by situations that fall into hazy ethical zones, much less the obvious situations that arise in which foregoing integrity may provide some immediate benefit. It's difficult to fight temptation, and most of us are unable to resist the lure of some immediate gratification, which ultimately separates the Warrior from the rest of the pack.

Although they should aspire to it, Warriors should not be arrogant enough to expect that they won't sometimes inadvertently step over this line, taking a position that jeopardizes their own integrity. Warriors make misjudgments and mistakes, and they sometimes blatantly fall for temptation and become momentary liars.

The key to maintaining Warrior status is how you react when the mistake is made. It's important to "own up" to the situation with those involved, and you should attempt to re-establish and earn credibility. This is and should be a painful process, because Warriors need to learn not to violate their integrity in the future. Warriors take responsibility, provide explanations, and try to right their wrongs. They don't have excuses. *Excuses are the most frequently used tools in the toolboxes of Whiners and Weasels, and they have no place in the Warrior's vocabulary.* As covered above, one of the keys to integrity is "making the hard call," especially when that call is to tell someone that despite your best efforts, you have failed to live up to your promise, but your goal is to right the situation.

Assess Your Own Integrity. Business situations and relationships change, often necessitating a change in plan from what was agreed upon earlier, and this can make it difficult for Warriors to accurately assess their own integrity. For instance, if you change your stance on an earlier position because of a radical change of events, have you violated your integrity? There is no way I can answer that question, as every situation has issues and nuances that a general rule can't cover.

However, communication and intent usually become key in these situations. Warriors typically have responsibilities to many different groups, e.g., their company, their clients, their coworkers, and their family. It's frequently difficult to serve all these masters while maintaining integrity. Ultimately, it's usually a question of staying faithful to the intent of your original agreement, and looking deep inside yourself to answer the question of whether or not you have violated your word.

Finally, this analysis must also examine whether or not you communicated sufficiently to all involved to maintain your integrity. One of the most unfortunate side effects of being a Warrior is that you must live with a certain level of self-analysis that can often be painful, but this analysis is a necessary step to "keep your tools tuned." Sometimes I find myself going to my wife or key managers for an "ethics check" when I'm unsure about how I should approach a situation.

#2: THE "I'LL MAKE IT HAPPEN" TOOL

Get out of a Warrior's way, because Warriors never give up, wear out, or take no for an answer.

Warriors Are Motivated. Warriors are an unbelievably motivated lot. They tend to have boundless energy and an enormous capacity for hard work. Unlike most people, they naturally assume that they will be successful at whatever they apply themselves to. Warriors are optimistic by their very nature, looking at every situation as a potential opportunity. This is one of the main reasons that Warriors frequently make such great entrepreneurs. Although others may look at a potential opportunity with a jaundiced eye, seeking only the reasons *not* to move forward, the Warrior sees the upside to the situation. This stands in stark contrast to the Whiner, who tends to view every situation as a potential problem.

Warriors Are Goal Oriented. For both short- and long-term goals, Warriors have the ability to stay so focused on achieving their goals that their success ratio is much higher than the rest of the population. If Warriors are unsuccessful, they naturally surmise they didn't work hard enough, and they resign themselves to do better on the next attempt. *This stands in stark contrast to most "non-Warriors," who usually find someone else to blame or some other excuse for their failure.*

Warriors Don't Burn Out. Warriors don't really understand the concept of "working too hard" or "burning out," until exhaustion legitimately begins to hamper their work. They never complain about their workload, as they see it all as an opportunity, and are usually just pleased that they are successful enough to have the work to perform. If they do believe that they are being treated unfairly or overworked in comparison to their compensation, they will go to their supervisors and clearly and calmly state their case, which usually has positive results. In contrast, non-Warriors spend a lot of time focusing on their perception of their workload, and often take the conflict avoider approach, complaining to coworkers, spouses, and friends about how unjust their situation is instead of dealing with the situation directly.

Warriors Work Harder and More Productively Than Others. In many respects, Warriors are usually more successful than others simply because they work harder and are more productive with their work time. This is not to say that the Warrior's life then becomes totally work-focused drudgery—because Warriors also tend to take this aggressive approach toward their free time: working hard to have the "best vacations" or being the best at their hobbies and other pleasurable pursuits. The most successful Warriors also tend to work smarter, eventually transitioning out of the long hours of their early career into shorter, more productive bursts of energy. This becomes an incredibly important point. I know many people who are great Workers or Warriors-on-the-cusp, but don't make the transition to Warrior because they are ineffective with their work time. They put in the hours, but even with the best of intentions don't get much done in relation to the effort they expend. In contrast, as Warriors get more skillful at using their tools, they can accomplish more in a shorter period of time.

Warriors Are Supremely Confident (and Sometimes Arrogant). Thanks in part to their driven personalities and constant state of confidence, Warriors also tend to be extremely aggressive and often confrontational at almost everything they do. Although this aggressiveness can often be annoying (and is frequently misunderstood and mislabeled by many, with four-letter and longer adjectives not appropriate for this book), the truth is that Warriors are always in a hurry, and they don't have time for delays or chit chat. They have learned that their aggressiveness usually gets them what they want, and like Pavlov's dogs, as their aggression is continually rewarded, they tend to maintain their aggressive ways. Hence, "no" is seldom (if ever) an acceptable response to a Warrior's request. They persevere until they get the desired response.

Warriors Know How to Negotiate to Get What They Want. This perseverance becomes one of the Warrior's most profitable tools. Utilizing this tool, Warriors also enjoy the process of negotiation, because they have learned that directly asking for what you want, and making a compelling case for why you should have it, almost always results in the achievement of your goal. They also understand that most people dislike or are not good at the negotiation process (particularly conflict avoiders), so it is a talent that makes them stand apart. Sometimes, Warriors make more money, have better jobs, and enjoy more perks in life primarily because they just asked for it, when non-Warriors were just too inhibited to make the request.

For example, a good friend of mine has enjoyed a successful career over the last two decades heading business divisions of several major corporations. One of the most interesting things about my friend's career is that he is consistently able to negotiate salary and benefit packages at his new jobs that are literally *double or even triple* what the comparable job normally pays! Although he has been a great asset to his companies and has always made them money, he is the consummate Warrior in his negotiations, filled with self-confidence and armed with the right kind of data that allows him to negotiate enormous salaries. Certainly, most people encounter these kinds of situations in their business lives, but the Warrior in a workplace somehow manages to negotiate a salary far above everyone else's level.

I have personally found that the confidence to negotiate is one of my most useful tools as a Warrior, and I consequently tend to negotiate almost everything in business and my day-to-day life. For instance, I always negotiate when a vendor's delivery falls below reasonable expectations. Most people would be amazed to discover that if you have the confidence to negotiate, almost everything is negotiable. Because I travel a lot and because I spend a lot of money in the process, I especially negotiate with travel vendors. I am a believer in the axiom that "you get what you pay for," and I don't mind paying the appropriate premium price for premium service, but I also find that given my continual travel budgets and the frequency of travel vendors to fall below promised standards, it is an area of constant negotiations. In the past few months, I have negotiated several free round-trip airline tickets from major airlines, several first-class upgrades, thousands of free frequent-flyer miles, and a $1,000 flight credit—all negotiated settlements when their service was far below expectations. I constantly negotiate and receive car rental free days and upgrades, free hotel nights and upgrades to suites, free meals or sometimes wine or cocktails with dinner . . . the list goes on and on.

I also negotiate for many of my normal purchases. For instance, the other day, I negotiated at a big box retail store for the purchase of light fixtures, saving almost $100. Last week, while buying a new watch for my wife at a high-end jewelry story, I negotiated 25 percent off the list price. Recently, when investing money into certified deposits at my bank, I easily negotiated a higher interest rate than publicized, just by making a call. I negotiated a reduction in my bill from the phone company because I was dissatisfied with the service. On my last purchase of a new car, I was able to negotiate more than $5,000 off the initial best price I was given. Again, the list goes on and on, and I estimate that as a result of my negotiations I easily save $10,000 or more per year!

The Warrior realizes that almost everything in life is negotiable (even in scenarios that you would not assume negotiation was possible), and that having the Warrior's confidence to negotiate opens doors, saves money, makes money, and allows the Warrior to generally live a better life than the non-Warrior.

But Beware of Taking These Warrior Traits Too Far. Of course, like many of the Warrior's tools, you can take the art of negotiation too far. Although you might be able to negotiate a lower price, a better deal, etc., the Warrior also needs to look at the bigger picture. Years ago, we were traveling with another couple overseas, and the man we were touring with (a strong and successful Warrior) went though a hard negotiation with a street vendor to save a few dollars. Though I knew it was his second-nature, and I have done similar negotiations in the past, I realized how ridiculous it was to beat up a poor street vendor to save a few dollars.

A lower price also may be negotiated in exchange for a lower level of service that ultimately ends up costing you more. Keep in mind that relationships are key to the Warrior, and it is short-term thinking to constantly be hammering on key relationships for a lower price. Relationships go both ways, and if you don't allow your key relationships to adequately profit from their interaction with you, those relationships will soon implode and your profitability will be impacted. Over the years, I have refused to work with many businesses that I think I could really assist—due to their reputations for "nickel and diming" their vendors. While they might find that approach a legitimate business approach, they also need to judge whether they would be more successful working with properly compensated vendors dedicated to their success, as opposed to companies working with such slim margins that they cannot afford to adequately service them. The ideal negotiation ends happily for both parties.

Also, too much success in negotiations can sometimes lead to failure. For example, many years ago, I negotiated to sell a company I owned. I had an interested buyer, and after a month of heavy negotiations, the buyer flew into town for dinner to hammer out a few final details. We agreed on a deal, the lawyers went to work on the final paperwork that evening, and we agreed to meet the next morning to sign the deal. Unfortunately, the buyer never showed up. When I reached him that afternoon, he had already taken a flight home. "You negotiated too good of a deal," he told me somewhat sheepishly. "Although I agreed in person, when I got back to my hotel, I felt you had run over me, and I just lost my incentive to do the deal."

As a result, I was in a terrible position to negotiate with other buyers because I had spent a month with him. Ultimately, the company sold for a fraction of the deal I almost did with the first buyer. Had I been a little less aggressive in the final negotiations, I would have made much more money and suffered a lot less stress.

Warriors Are Demanding of Others—and They Need to Know When to Let Up. As the saying goes, Warriors also "don't suffer fools lightly." Warriors are not only demanding of themselves, but also of those they work with. This puts the Warrior's team at a decisive advantage over non-Warrior competition, because they typically are just a more talented and driven group. However, this can make life in the Warrior's shadow difficult for the Workers on their team.

Therefore, Warriors needs to be on constant guard not to let their aggressive and confrontational personalities overwhelm themselves and the people around them. I've met many Warriors over the years who allowed this potentially dark personality trait to develop too much (in fact, I personally have to keep this tool in check above all the others). They end up becoming a caricature of the Warrior: unhappy, screaming bosses who constantly berate everyone around them, driving people to unnatural pursuits of unnecessary perfection and creating unhappy environments. This is a trait that I personally battle more than most. It is a fine balance between having high expectations and driving those around you to share those expectations because of your aggressiveness and robbing those of incentive by pushing too hard.

Used judiciously, this "I'll-make-it-happen tool" is one of the most powerful tools in the Warrior's box, but used improperly, it can easily ruin Warriors and the Workers who surround them. Warriors should always emote power, holding the respect of those around them, and clearly communicating the subtle but direct threat to the Weasels of the world that they "should not fool with you," because as a Warrior, you will fight back. But maintaining a constant state of anger doesn't achieve this goal, and it often sends the wrong messages to the valuable Workers. I advise Warriors to take a periodic "drive and aggression" tune-up. Stand back and look at yourself from an anger-free perspective to make sure you aren't punishing the Workers in your effort to eradicate the Weasels.

For many Warriors, the drive and aggression tool can be a valid replacement for intelligence or even talent. Society, business, politics, and the history books are full of Warriors who saw their vision to successful fruition not because they were great innovators or intellects, but simply because they refused to accept "no" as the answer. They persevered long after most people would give up.

Also, not ever accepting "no" as an answer is certainly one of the most crucial personality attributes of the Warrior. Most people give up the fight long before the Warrior would ever consider quitting. Drive and "no is never no" also give Warriors a decisive advantage in any negotiation, because they usually just persevere longer than their opponents, often simply wearing them down until the Warrior receives the outcome he or she desires. And unlike the more prevalent conflict avoiders, Warriors love to negotiate. They use their drive and aggression to constantly negotiate almost everything in their lives.

This drive and aggression is probably one of the most misunderstood and frequently disliked tools by non-Warriors. Although most people seek a balance in their lives, Warriors are often fixated on specific goal achievement, and it is difficult for them to understand why everyone they are around would not share the same goal and be willing to totally dedicate themselves to it like the Warrior does.

Hence, it is easy for Warriors to "burn out" those around them. Warrior managers need to be cognizant of the fact that not everyone shares their drive, and their organization should also include Workers who are devoted to their jobs, but who also make their families and/or outside interests an equal priority to the achievement of specific business goals. It's imperative that Warrior managers understand the motivations of the non-Warriors in their workplace and that they temper their teams accordingly.

#3: THE SELF-RESPONSIBILITY TOOL

"Warriors take the credit, and the blame." Self-responsibility is a vital component in the Warrior's toolbox, as it is one of the main traits that immediately and obviously separate the Warrior from Workers, Whiners, and Weasels. Warriors take complete responsibility for everything good and bad that happens in their lives. There are no excuses for failure, just explanations that become learning experiences to improve performance in the future. *Warriors acknowledge that regardless of their backgrounds, education, financial situations, and other issues that might be perceived as initial advantages or disadvantages, they ultimately possess free will, so they ultimately control the good or bad that occurs in their lives.*

Great Warriors have come from horrific backgrounds, just as world-class Weasels have descended from society's most elite and privileged ranks. And although wealth, education, and other early advantages can certainly smooth the way, ultimately it is the Warrior's mind-set that sees him or her through to success.

Warriors Admit Their Past Mistakes. This particular tool (or the lack thereof) makes it quick and easy to spot the Warrior versus the non-Warrior in a job setting or in a personal setting. In conversation, or in more formalized situations such as a job interview, non-Warriors typically spend a lot of time assessing blame on others for their situation or lack of success.

They will discuss ad nauseam how a family situation, previous boss, spouse, coworker, parent, sibling, or other factor in their life has held them back. They are society's victims, usually expressing complete lack of control over the situations that brought them to present-day. They fail to acknowledge that once they reached adulthood, they made their own choices about their direction, their associations, and other factors that determined their current situation.

And worst of all, their inability to accept responsibility has much more far-reaching societal implications. They clog our legal system with frivolous actions designed to penalize everyone else for their situations. They slow productivity by concentrating on why things don't work, instead of how to make them work better.

In contrast, Warriors may point out difficulties in their pasts, but they will always acknowledge their mistakes—and the solutions they sought to improve the situations. Warriors who have not reached their goals will ask for opportunities—the simple chance to prove themselves—because they possess the Warrior's confidence, and they know that simply being given the opportunity is the first step to control their destiny and achieve their goals. In contrast, the non-Warrior seeks guarantees of stability, as opposed to opportunity.

Warriors Want Rewards Tied to Their Performance. Here is another quick "Warrior vs. non-Warrior" test. In a professional environment, Warriors always prefer to work on some kind of incentive-based compensation (e.g., commission, performance bonus, etc.) that is directly tied to individual performance. In contrast, non-Warriors prefer a more stable salary, or a bonus that is tied to group performance, so they can't be held individually accountable.

Warriors Never Rely on Luck. Although they may acknowledge that they were blessed with favorable timing in a situation, Warriors understand that they ultimately control their own destiny, and their success or failure is a reflection of their choices and performance.

In contrast, many Workers, Whiners, and Weasels spend their entire lives living a "lottery lifestyle," a concept I touched on briefly in chapter 1 and will continue to talk about through the book. The lottery lifestyle is a philosophy built on the foundation that success in life is more a function of luck than talent or the use of the Warrior's tools. Those living the lottery lifestyle frequently point at the circumstances surrounding someone else's success, as opposed to the fact that most people who are successful got that way by working hard and utilizing their talents to the best of their ability.

So, from the perspective of someone living the lottery lifestyle, Bill Gates is the richest man in the world because he happened to be in the right place at the right time—at the intersection of IBM and the dawning of personal computers. They would never surmise that he was actually instrumental in formulating this new age and that he is a brilliant visionary and businessman, and deserves his success. This would imply to people living the lottery lifestyle that they are destined to stay in their current situations unless they personally effect some change—a fact they don't want to hear. Instead, they prefer to believe that "their ship will come in" in the form of literally winning the lottery, owning a stock that takes off, having a great weekend in Vegas, getting "rear-ended" by someone wealthy who quickly offers a huge settlement, or some other form of luck that puts no personal responsibility on them.

People who hold these beliefs often tend to under-perform in their day-to-day lives. Instead of really applying themselves to improve their situation—perhaps earn a promotion, bonus, or some other incentive-based bonus based on their performance—they instead prefer to offer minimal effort, complain about their lot in life, and wait for the big payoff they think they deserve. American society is especially susceptible to the lottery lifestyle right now. The incredible stock market performance of the last decade, the real estate surge of this decade, and the instant millionaires and billionaires created by the technology boom have given people the misconception that wealth and success are easily achievable and almost a birthright for all. This is compounded by the barrage of reality shows that offer instant fame and wealth to a select few who did nothing but make it through the casting process. We also find the successful and wealthy a form of entertainment, with reality shows highlighting the rich and the chosen few they may deign to make rich, which then supports the incorrect belief that we all deserve success.

While Warriors are supremely optimistic about their own success, they realize there is no easy road to achieving it. Warriors take a long-term value approach toward the future, and although they will certainly attempt to take advantage of market conditions, they build a stable base.

Warriors Face Problems Head On. The Warrior also understands that to be successful, it is essential to take responsibility when problems do occur, make the necessary changes to improve performance in the future, pay any appropriate penalty for mistakes that were made, and finally move on. Often, Warriors-on-the-cusp will spend too long lamenting and analyzing a situation gone wrong, instead of just moving on. Pay the price, but don't pay it twice, and move on to success. Consider the mistake, and the pain it caused, a kind of tuition payment to make sure you don't repeat what you did wrong.

#4: THE INTUITION TOOL

Your gut is your biggest ally. This is one of the most important—but perhaps most difficult—tools to use in the Warrior's toolbox. Unfortunately, you are either blessed with good intuition—or you aren't. Intuition cannot be taught; all I can do in this book is encourage you to access and understand the power of your intuition, trust it, and if it is one of your working tools, encourage you to use it.

Warriors Know What's the Right Thing to Do. Most Warriors possess a keen sense of the right action to take in almost any situation they confront (although it is still possible to have average or below-average intuition and still be a Warrior, if the rest of your tools are highly developed). Possessing good intuition is only part of the challenge; having the courage to use it is often the most difficult part of the process. Sometimes, your intuition will tell you that you have to make a difficult decision that on the surface may not look appropriate.

For instance, your intuition may tell you to avoid a potentially lucrative client or business deal, or not to hire a potentially talented employee. Good intuition takes many forms, but one of the Warrior's best uses of intuition is to spot Weasels. A Weasel business partner, vendor, employee, coworker, client, or a personal relationship with a Weasel can represent an enormous drain on emotional and financial resources. Having the intuitive sense to spot the Weasel in advance and quickly take the appropriate action is a huge benefit. Almost without exception, anytime I have disregarded my intuition throughout my career, I have ended up making a mistake. On a few occasions, I ignored my intuition when it told me that a particular business investment was sound, and almost without exception, these missed opportunities have experienced incredible increases in value. Over the years, I went against my intuition on three memorable occasions when dealing with the hiring of key employees, and on all three occasions I ended up hiring Weasels who cost me untold heartache and personal aggravation, wasted time, and potentially millions of dollars.

On many occasions, I have disregarded my intuition in regard to clients, trusting them to pay a bill or follow through on a promise when my intuition said it would not happen, and in almost every case, I ended up losing money. And in most of these situations, when I analyzed why I ignored my intuition, there was one simple reason—greed. I took the calculated risk of dealing with a Weasel in the hope of bigger profits, and I ended up losing. Ignoring your intuition and trusting a Weasel is a bad odds bet.

Warriors Trust Their Intuition. Even when you feel you have really honed your Warrior tools and skills, it is still easy to doubt your intuition. For example, a few years ago, a CEO of a company made the decision to bring in a new CFO. On paper and initially in person, "Lurch"[1] as I will call him (in tribute to the character in *The Addams Family* TV show) seemed to be perfect for the job. (You will get to meet Lurch in detail later in the Weasel section of the book.) He had a strong financial background, talked a good game, and, at first, seemed to be a consensus builder among the staff.

However, within a few weeks, the CEO intuitively knew something was wrong. Lurch started exhibiting overly competitive traits that immediately spelled "WEASEL," with capital letters. He immediately attempted to build "camps" within the organization to isolate any groups— and especially any Warriors—that he thought were not supportive of his

---

1. Throughout the book, I have changed names to protect the "not-so-innocent" and a few truly innocent souls who probably don't want to be discussed here.

goals. He filled key positions with "yes men" who blindly supported anything he said.

But Lurch was a hard worker, and he certainly was competent at many of his duties. When asked, the employees had nothing but positive things to say about Lurch. Ultimately, Lurch ravaged the company.

Within a few months, he had turned the operation upside down, built dissent among the board, and pushed the company in a direction that cost the shareholders millions of dollars. And the bottom line? It was the CEO's fault for not trusting his instincts.

Often intuition is just highly developed "Weasel radar," which can be extremely beneficial to Workers as well as Warriors. If your intuition is telling you not to trust the person you are dealing with, chances are you should forego the enticing benefits of the relationship, because you are most likely right.

And in this age of "corporate research," where business decisions are usually modeled, paraded out before focus groups, tested, and overanalyzed, a Warrior's good intuition will still win out as the best guidepost for a company to follow in its development. Once you have established that your intuition is sound, you should follow it without hesitation, because in the long run, it will serve you well.

#5: THE PERSONAL BRAND TOOL

Your reputation precedes you. A successful Warrior (and, for that matter, a Worker) ultimately develops a personal brand. (Please note that the concept of "personal brand" is not something I originated; it has been espoused by others in business circles. I just find it to be an essential Warrior tool.) Just as you trust that BMW is synonymous with world-class automobiles, that Wal-Mart means low prices, and that Nike shoes feature an athletic heritage, style, and quality—so should you have a positive "personal brand" that is synonymous with you and how you use your tools. Your personal brand (assuming it is positive) should precede you into many business and social situations. Regardless of where you fall in the scope of the Four W's, you will have a personal brand whether you like it or not, so it is always best to take control and hone it in a positive way.

If you live life as a Warrior and utilize the Warrior's tools, you will develop a personal brand that is partially based on the integrity, honesty, and drive that are a regular part of your life. That is one of the advantages of being a Warrior—you tap into an existing positive basis for your personal brand, almost like buying into a franchise. But past this point, you should endeavor to develop a unique and compelling component of your personal brand that really separates you from the masses. Your personal brand might be simple, e.g., "Extremely Reliable," or "Willing to Put in the Extra Work to Make a Project Really Special." Or it can be more complex—e.g., "A Great Asset on Complex Deals."

Warriors Constantly Improve Their Personal Brand. It's essential to take an accurate periodic assessment of your personal brand to make sure it hasn't taken a wrong turn—and to constantly try to find ways to improve your brand. Companies such as Procter & Gamble, which has built one of the world's most successful companies based on mega-brands like Tide and Dove, understand how essential it is to periodically tune up a brand—hence, the many "new and improved" advertisements that fill the airwaves.

I've had the opportunity to work with many world-class product and personal brands over the years, and the successful ones go to tremendous lengths to protect and enhance their brand. Great brands understand that it is essential to reinforce their brand message in every way they interact with the consumer. You should take the same approach to your personal brand—taking care to protect and enhance it—and to make sure that it remains consistent.

Your Personal Brand Becomes Your Reputation—Good or Bad. A personal brand establishes others' expectations of you even before they meet you, and if that brand is positive, it can expedite business deals and relationships. Warriors have personal brands like the following:

- "Nice person to deal with—always dependable"
- "Best salesman I've ever met"
- "Always keeps his word"
- "Incredible follow-up"
- "Smart and gets to the point"

- "Always does great work"
- "Great at customer service"

and even

- "Tough, but smart and fair"
- "Hope you don't have to compete against her because she is good"
- "Picky and a bit difficult to deal with—but the end result is always worth it"
- "An artist"
- "Great date—a good listener and sexy"

These personal brands are all extremely beneficial calling cards to proceed you into any business or personal relationship.

A personal brand can also be enticing via a built-in selectivity that people find alluring such as:

- "Expensive, but if you want the best, they are worth it"
- "Temperamental—but a genius"
- "Slow—but the best and worth waiting for"

And, of course, a negative personal brand can have the opposite effect. Consider how many people you've met with personal brands like:

- "Doesn't pay his bills"
- "Constantly overpromises"
- "Terrible date—cheap with bad breath"
- "Way too expensive for what you receive"
- "Self-centered—always talks about himself and never listens"
- "Be careful—a real backstabber"
- "Nice guy—but a terrible gossip"
- "Arrogant and hard to work with"

● "A real weasel"

Sometimes, accomplished Warriors develop bad personal brands without even knowing it, for relatively minor offenses that are major in their respective industries and situations. For instance, I have a friend, a consummate Warrior in many respects, who is the president of a successful product marketing company. One of his company's biggest challenges and expenses is locating new products. It spends millions per year advertising, attending trade shows, and calling on companies and inventors in an attempt to find new products.

But the problem begins after the company attracts the attention. Unbeknownst to my friend, he had developed the personal brand "Never returns phone calls and slow to do a deal." After spending a fortune to attract new products, he chased them away through his lack of follow-up. Although he was aware that he had a reputation for not returning phone calls, he did not take it seriously at first. As a result, he was losing several deals a year, and he was wasting a tremendous amount of effort and marketing capital because his negative brand preceded him.

How to Solve a Problem with a Negative Personal Brand. After I explained the impact of my friend's personal brand, the easy solution was for him to hire a competent assistant, whose primary purpose was to constantly return phone calls on his behalf and to keep clients apprised of developments pertaining to their deals. Although having someone make contact for you is not a full replacement for personal contact, in his case, it did solve a lot of problems that were hampering his organization. A $28,000-per-year expense for the assistant changed his personal brand, resulting in millions per year in savings and added revenues.

Executives frequently develop bad brands simply because they are too busy to handle the necessary details to keep their brand shining, so it's important to be cognizant of these issues, and if necessary and possible assign someone else to assist with some of the duties—sort of like a personal brand manager. Executives who are weak in certain areas should make sure their assistant has the skill set to bolster those areas in which they don't shine. Too often I have seen executives hire weak assistants that actually hurt their brand.

My assistant has been a great asset as part of my personal brand team. When I hired her, I explained some of the basic platforms of my personal brand that we both needed to adhere to. A few examples include:

- Our friendly "high touch" treatment of clients and vendors begins from the first time they call or communicate with us and continues throughout our relationship.

- All communication from clients or business partners will be returned within twenty-four hours—preferably within the same eight-hour day.

- All written and telephone communications follows a kind of "style book" that reflects the brand—for instance, make sure there are no misspellings and that letters and e-mails are formatted to be consistent with an approved design.

- Treat everyone as respectfully as possible. The annoying salesperson trying to get our business might some day be a client.

- We maintain a "personal communication" strategy with employees and clients so that I can stay in touch as much as possible.

- We never take no for an answer when we are seeking something important until every possible option to achieve success has been exhausted.

- We always attempt to get maximum value from our transactions.

My wife Michelle also plays an important role in my personal brand maintenance. Since we also work together professionally, she gets to see me in action (sometimes much to her dismay), and she can be much more direct with me than my employees. She is quick to point out when I need a little brand tune-up due to my mishandling of situations. Having someone in your life that can be really direct (as in Michelle yelling, "You're acting like a Whiner") and forthright about how you might be slipping can be a great asset.

Often, a small investment in improving a personal brand will eliminate costly problems in other parts of your life or business, resulting in a major overhaul in cost savings and/or profitability.

Be Aware of Your Personal Brand. Frequently, an individual's personal and professional life intersect, often resulting in negative and sometimes unjustified personal brands. Although these bad personal brands start out as malicious gossip (and Weasel competitors will often take this tack), you do need to be aware of what is happening to control it. Personal brands are much like product brands—they can often unjustifiably be harmed by consumer perception and even just out-and-out lies, and it is the individual's responsibility to control his or her brand.

Consider the example of a president of a mid-sized company, who works hard and doesn't get much time to vacation. When he attends the two large industry conventions every year, he utilizes the opportunity to take a few extra days off and really "let loose." Unfortunately, others in the industry have seen him "letting loose," which has included making drunken, late-night excursions to the hotel hot tub, leading loud and nearly incomprehensible singing in hotel bars and restaurants, and other activities that would be much more acceptable while vacationing with friends at a beachside resort than at a trade show. As a result, his personal brand in the industry contains the words "wild drunk," which certainly doesn't attract the kind of clientele most want.

Although you should enjoy your work—and I think it's extremely valuable for a personal brand to contain adjectives like "fun," "entertaining," "a good person to spend an evening with"—it is important to isolate any aspects of your life from your brand that might be taken out of context and come to haunt you. The president who lets loose at conventions needs to head to Cabo when he wants to relax and let his hair down, and keep his business trips a little more business-focused for his own good.

Your Personal Brand Can Help Your Company, Too. Many of the world-class companies we are all familiar with are simply extensions of the founder's personal brand, so entrepreneurs need to be acutely aware of their personal brands. For example, when you read about Sam Walton, founder of Wal-Mart and at the time of his death one of the richest men in history, the articles usually talk about Walton's homespun ways and conservative lifestyle. Wal-Mart's brand of "great values from nice folks" and Sam Walton's personal brand are ultimately one and the same. The articles will often point out that Walton usually drove a ten-year-old pickup instead of an ultra-expensive luxury car that he could certainly afford, and despite all his riches, he particularly enjoyed time in the country with his family. He believed in value, as do his stores. Those that make the trip to Bentonville to deal with Wal-Mart will confirm that his personal brand and the company brand remain one and the same, as the headquarters is a no-frills place and employees adopt a low-key persona. Now, I don't know if Walton's image was true, or a figment of a great publicist's imagination, but I suspect that Walton probably often drove his truck to the airport to board his private jet. Walton's personal brand worked well for him and his company.

At the opposite end of the spectrum, you have a businessman like Donald Trump, whose overriding personal brand is *success*—and accordingly, his personal brand works. People who don't like Trump, and who therefore took pleasure in his financial troubles of a few years ago, usually have to grudgingly admit admiration at his resurrection as a real estate mogul.

A few months ago, I was riding in a cab in New York City. As we passed a new Trump building, the cabbie made the comment, "There's another of Donald's palaces." I inquired as to his opinion of Trump, and the cabbie replied that he "loved the guy. He gets stuff done. The city of New York couldn't even get an ice-skating rink built, and Trump took over the project and got it done in half the time for half the dough. I like guys that get stuff done." The cabbie concluded, "I'd even vote for the guy for president."

Like him or not, part of Trump's personal brand is "gets it done" and "never gives up"—both admirable and appropriate personal brands for a Warrior. Most positive personal brands are, to a great extent, a reflection of how one utilizes the integrity tool, and in some way, they revolve around "doing what you say you're going to do."

Your Personal Brand Includes Your Image and How You Look. In business, it's also important to consider the impact your "look" has on your personal brand, as it shouldn't interfere with your message. Your image can be used to your tremendous advantage if you know how to control it. Now, I know many people particularly hate this part of the personal brand message, because we would all prefer to think that how we look should not impact our success, but unfortunately, that just isn't the way it works.

Good or bad, we all make our initial judgments based on appearance. People often unwittingly let a bad hairstyle or an unflattering wardrobe get in the way of their message. Like it or not, if you are overweight or have highly unusual features or physical characteristics, people are going to have perceptions or misconceptions about you—that's just a problem you will have to deal with. Also, a look that is too slick or inconsistent with other parts of your personal brand can cause problems. A farm-implement salesman with greased-backed hair and dressed in a high-fashion suit most likely would not inspire confidence in his clientele.

Although perhaps it is sad that image is so important, the Warrior is aware of all these issues and deals with them. For example, I have two friends who work as account executives at an advertising agency. One is certainly competent at her job, but she's not at all a star performer, just very much a competent Worker. However, she has a great flair for style. Her hair and wardrobe, although not exorbitantly expensive, make a nice statement to clients expecting their advertising agency to be a little "hip." She knows the best restaurants to take a client to and the ideal place for a drink afterwards.

The other account executive, on the other hand, is much more competent at her job (in fact, she is a Warrior-rising). She works hard, and once her clients get to know her, they love her. But she hasn't updated her wardrobe or hair since John Travolta had a television series. "So I'm a granola," she explains, "I like to look this way." That is certainly her right, and I applaud her choice as long as she is comfortable with the results, but the fact is, due to this issue, she has not risen through the ranks the way she should. Management is concerned about the first impression she makes on a client, so she only works on established accounts, which minimizes her opportunities.

The fact is, company management has a right to make sure that employees in positions that have a lot of client interface reflect accurately the company's brand, and anyone who wants to progress within an organization would do themselves a favor by analyzing their company's brand and making sure they are in sync with it. Once again, it might not be fair, but it is reality, and Warriors deal with reality or change it so it works for them.

I personally have several wardrobes, each tailored for the type of client or individual with whom I am negotiating. Although each of them communicates the essence of my personal brand, I dress differently, for instance, for a group of conservative Midwesterners, than I do for a New York audience. Some may complain that this approach is disingenuous, but the fact is that in business all brands undergo slight alterations to better appeal to their target demographic, while still maintaining their core brand equity. Procter & Gamble's advertising in Mexico looks different than its advertising in New York City, but the core of the message is the same.

Managing Your Personal Brand. Great companies realize that managing their brands requires making sure the brand is consistent in every contact they have with a consumer. Individuals should also think about this in managing their personal brand. Do your e-mails, letters, even the message on your voice mail reflect how you want people to regard you? For example, a friend of mine—a law school-educated, high-level business executive—consistently sends out e-mails that are riddled with misspellings and grammatical errors. Although I love the guy and know what a brilliant fellow he is, I cannot help but wince every time I get an e-mail from him. His bad writing skills or his laziness in just not using a spell checker cast a pall on an otherwise wonderful personal brand.

Your Personal Brand Mirrors Your Integrity. Certainly, there are components of your personal brand that never change under any circumstances. They are usually core to your integrity, and your integrity tools should stay consistent throughout your life. The development of your personal brand should never take you to a point where you are forced to sacrifice your integrity. A position that requires you to change your positive core beliefs, or mask your cultural, racial, or sexual identity is a position that should be avoided, as it espouses Weasel action.

But the Warrior also realizes that there are certain aspects to the brand that fall more into the realm of "theater," and there is no reason not to use those components to your advantage. Ideally, a personal brand is a statement of core beliefs that most likely never change, and the less-important "surface appearances" of the brand that Warriors use to their advantage may vary by situation.

#6: THE RELATIONSHIP TOOL

All of the above tools, if properly utilized and maintained, will result in a Warrior establishing a variety of valuable relationships that ultimately become one of the most dependable and powerful tools in the box. When a Warrior with a positive personal brand leaves his or her position with a company, it is almost always more traumatic for the company than the Warrior. Warriors have the self-confidence, toolbox, and relationships to move to a job as good as or better than the one they left, but the company is left with a big void to fill. Relationships are always primarily "person to person," and good relationships are a Warrior's (and company's) greatest assets. In contrast, company-to-company relationships are always temporary and unstable.

Your Network Is Critical to Your Success. For example, when I start a new company now, it is not only much easier for me than it was twenty years ago because I am more experienced, better capitalized, and (hopefully) smarter—but also because I have a network of relationships that I can tap into. When I vacation or travel now, I almost always have a network of connections and/or relationships around the world ready to show me the sites, recommend a restaurant, or come to my aid if necessary. Many of these relationships are with other Warriors, but it's essential to have connections that extend far beyond the "Warrior-to-Warrior" world.

These relationships stay in place at first glance because of my personal brand, and my personal brand is a conglomeration of my use of my Warrior tools. But it takes more than just a positive personal brand to maintain long-term relationships. You must make a concerted effort to communicate with some regularity with those who have impacted your day-to-day life. There is sometimes a temptation not to communicate with people for fear you will disturb them, and certainly you can't build relationships if you are really just a pest that people don't want to hear from. But the reality is that most people welcome contact from old friends and business associates they enjoy being around, and Warriors cannot let their own potential shyness keep them from developing relationships.

Technology Makes It Easy to Maintain Contact with Your Network. Luckily, technology has never made it easier to establish some form of easy communication, via e-mail and faxes. Regular communication also can vary tremendously, and I am certainly not advocating that a busy businessperson spend his or her entire day communicating with everyone he or she comes in contact with. (I also am not a fan of those "joke chain letters" that seem to be in endless circulation. Putting a friend or business associate on a time-wasting electronic junk mail list does not equate to communicating to maintain a relationship!) I have people with whom I only communicate every several years; others I contact once a year; and, of course, others with whom I speak on a weekly or even daily basis.

I make it a regular practice to maintain communication, and the truth is, it is one of my favorite aspects of my life. For my personal friends, I take time to make calls, drop notes, schedule lunches, or keep in touch in some way. Often, though it may seem awkward, it is rewarding. A few years ago, on a whim, I tracked down an old friend I had not seen in almost twenty years, and once we were both past the embarrassment of going so long without contact, we rebuilt a wonderful relationship that we now maintain.

In my business, I also utilize tools like a short periodic "e-mail newsletter" that contains useful current industry data. I send it to a list of current clients and industry contacts. I also regularly clip appropriate articles from publications and send them with a personal note to appropriate parties. I regularly send messages, cards, and/or gifts on client's and special contact's birthdays or for special events. This type of communication can almost be "automated" within your organization, with the contact list ever expanding. For the minimal amount of time and effort it takes, it pays huge dividends.

Don't Ignore Your Relationships Because You're "Too Busy." Unfortunately, many of us fail to realize the value of accumulated relationships, and given today's especially mobile society, we move from job to job or personal relationship to personal relationship, frequently discarding the contacts and friends we've made along the way. This is a big mistake. Even though relationships you've built in your current job at first glance might not seem to be valuable in your new position, you will be surprised at how good relationships transcend industries. And keep in mind that relationships at every level can be important.

For example, early in my career, I made relationships while working in the petroleum equipment business—certainly one of the furthest possible industries from e-commerce and advertising that I now work in—but twenty years later, I still consistently find that some of the contacts I made early in my career are still active and valuable. Currently, one of my company's largest accounts came to us as result of a relationship I forged five years ago with the vice president of the company while he was at another company. Accordingly, it is essential that you regard everyone you come into contact with as having the potential to interface with you for the rest of your life.

Invest in Your Relationships. Regard your relationships as you would a bank or investment account. They should be guarded and added to on a regular basis, and they will pay dividends. If you find your "bank balance" of relationships declining, make the effort to build it up. Your good relationships will make introductions to new relationships, and your relationship account will grow. I regard my relationship account as one of my single most valuable assets—in many ways more important than money.

Treat Everyone Equally. It is also a mistake to attempt to constantly judge the *value* of each relationship and to only put your effort toward those that would most immediately benefit you. Aside from the fact that this quickly builds a negative personal brand, it is also a shortsighted approach toward life and business. Keep in mind that most of today's celebrities, billionaires, and other powerful people used to work in parking lots, bookstores, and other low-level jobs (perhaps waiting on you). The funny-looking guy parking your car might be tomorrow's Bill Gates, so you don't want him to remember you as the "jerk who was always yelling."

It doesn't take any extra effort to offer a kind word to those you contact in your day-to-day life, building a relationship that can then be deposited in your bank account. Deposits, no matter how small, add up. And the kind words offer the benefit of an immediate payback to those delivering them, because there is certainly a good feeling from making someone else smile.

#7: THE "TALK IS CHEAP" TOOL

Warriors don't pontificate about what they are going to do; they discuss what they've actually done.

All the above tools are worthless if not used, and one of the most important differences between a Warrior and a non-Warrior is simply *action*. The first step toward "getting the deal," "finding the perfect relationship," "improving your situation," and "getting a better job" is as basic as taking action. As simple as this sounds, it is extremely difficult for most people. They *think* about taking action, *plan* to take action, but they never actually make the steps, for a wide variety of reasons.

What You Do Is Critical to Your Success. Warriors are ultimately judged by the success of their actions, so it is only natural to them that they would be in almost perpetual motion. And it is lack of action that ultimately separates the Warrior from the Worker or the Whiner. Workers may legitimately decide not to take certain actions that would move them into a Warrior's position, because of the impact on the rest of their life. This is certainly a valid approach, for there is nothing wrong with being a satisfied Worker. The key to the Four W's is finding your comfort zone (without being a Whiner or Weasel).

For instance, for several years, I had a brilliant chief financial officer working for me. I had great plans for him as the organization progressed, but at a certain point in the company's development, he came to me and announced that he would be resigning within the next six months, and he would make the transition as easy as possible for the company. "I am only really interested in working for a company until it reaches a certain size," he announced, "because when it grows past that point, it would interfere with the time I want to spend with my family." He was a wonderful "former Warrior turned Worker" who had established his priorities and decided not to take any actions that would jeopardize the lifestyle he really enjoyed, and I had tremendous respect that he was sticking to his plan.

Warriors Talk—and Act. In contrast, Warriors don't concentrate on *talking* about what they are going to do—they spend their time *doing* it.

Don't Become a Blowhard. Here's another important aspect to this tool. Talk "really is cheap," and the Warrior needs to be careful not to diminish the value of talk even more by overutilizing it! I start or interrupt many internal meetings with the slogan **"TALK LESS—SAY MORE,"** which I think is extremely important advice for everyone. Unfortunately, many people tend to be bad listeners, with inflated opinions about the interest the crowd has for their stories.

It's important to participate and add valuable input, but in business and social situations, you always need to be aware of the fine line between entertaining conversation, valuable input, and "just noise."

Avoid "Analysis Paralysis." Many non-Warriors also suffer from "analysis paralysis," which causes them to overanalyze a situation, as opposed to just taking the appropriate action, or often any action at all. This affliction has unfortunately also infected many major corporations. I consistently see mid- and upper-level corporate executives who will do anything possible to avoid making an accountable decision that would lead to action, for fear the action will be unsuccessful. In contrast, Warriors understand that advancement only comes through action, and if they don't make the decision, they are destined to remain a Worker.

This lack of action and analysis paralysis can eventually cripple a company, as Warriors will leave for situations not so laden with fear and politics. As a result, once-great companies wither and die. For example, eighty years ago, W.W. Woolworth was one of the most powerful retailers in the world. It paid cash to build one of the biggest buildings in New York at the time, and today, it doesn't even exist. The company failed to take the necessary actions to keep pace with the market, and it paid the price.

Lack of action and analysis paralysis also can lead to expensive delays and missed opportunities. For example, a few years ago, I was working with a major company to introduce a new line of women's cosmetics. I told the client that it would cost approximately $500,000 to produce an advertising and marketing campaign to judge whether or not the product would be successful in wide distribution. The client informed me that it was company policy to first do research on the viability of the product. Essentially, the product manager preferred to follow the company guidebook instead of making a decision.

Instead of actually taking proactive action to test the product with consumers, the company spent an inordinate amount on consulting fees and focus groups in a laboratory setting to find out if consumers would buy. The "analysis" took so long that the market opportunity was over by the time the company decided to test the campaign, and the company not only wasted its money, but it also missed an opportunity to capitalize on a market worth hundreds of millions of dollars per year. Rather than take a Warrior's position, and risk testing its concept, this company preferred to spend the same amount of money the "safe" way, so if it failed, it didn't really fail: the research just showed it wouldn't work. Of course, although this kind of attitude may be safe, it also prevents success.

Warriors Make Things Happen. Warriors are crucial to society because they take the actions that make things happen. Although they might not always be the scientists who invent the miracle drug, they are the ones who make sure the drug reaches the masses. Although they might not invent the best possible software for your computer, they are the ones who make computers accessible to everyone. Although *action without forethought* is always a bad idea, it is always preferable to *great planning with no action*.

#8: THE TRUST TOOL

Find those you can trust, follow their advice, and most of all, strive to be someone who is trusted.

Although Warriors may be a bit suspicious by nature, and most would never be described as "trusting," successful Warriors do constantly seek out those with knowledge, instincts, and acumen that they personally do not possess. There is usually a collaborative aspect to most Warriors' successes—they know that to reach beyond a certain point, they require the help of others. Great companies are built on the fact that the founders, at least in the beginning, trusted each other and operated as a team. They extended the trust to their key employees, who then entrusted others to aid in the expansion. Trust is one of the reasons there are so many great family-owned companies, because despite how Aaron Spelling may portray family-run businesses on television, a family/business environment is usually much more conducive to trust, which allows for easier expansion.

Hire People You Can Trust. Of course, the key to all of this is finding people who are truly trustworthy, and unfortunately, the huge population of sneaky Weasels lurking around makes this difficult. In later chapters I will detail some Weasel-proofing techniques. There is certainly nothing wrong about withholding trust until someone earns your confidence—in fact, it should be standard practice. You also should not be surprised or insulted if someone places the same demands on you before delivering their trust. If you use your integrity tool properly, the trust of others will be a natural by-product.

The key for Warriors is making an honest assessment of their personal talents, and seeking out those who are trustworthy and who can supplement a Warrior's expertise with a new level of competence. I know many talented individuals who are stuck in a personal and professional "low gear" because they do not have the capacity to find trustworthy people who complement them well. Big success and personal happiness require the interaction of others.

#9: THE GUIDEPOST AND REWARD TOOL

After all is said and done, Warriors need a guidepost to judge their success and periodic rewards for all their good work.

Warriors Continually Measure—and Celebrate—Their Successes. Warriors know that all action inevitably leads to an outcome, and it's especially important that Warriors establish some kind of measurement tool to tell them when they are reaching their goals. Otherwise, they run the risk of constant discontent—always dissatisfied because, without an established goal, they can never tell when they have reached their objective. Because Warriors are so driven and motivated, they can sometimes get caught up in their own energy, forgetting why they are working so hard and striving so hard to succeed. Warriors need to periodically step back and take pride in their accomplishments (and the accomplishments of those around them) and celebrate their successes.

This celebration may be simple or quite grandiose. For example, I know Warriors who benchmark their successes by buying themselves rewards as they achieve certain goals, ranging from a nice reward dinner to the much more elaborate "I will buy that Porsche or take that vacation if I close this account."

Personally, I like to mark the achievement of certain professional and personal goals with treats ranging from a special bottle of wine for a minor victory to a vacation with my wife or an exotic fly-fishing excursion for a major achievement. When I first started my career, I promised myself that when I reached a certain point of financial success, I would reward myself with a country home on a river, where I could escape on the weekend with my family to recharge, fish, and enjoy the company of family and friends. A few years ago, I achieved that goal, and now I not only constantly enjoy the home, but it is also a motivator to keep working toward my future goals. My wife is also a Warrior, and we often set a joint guidepost to track our individual successes and our success as a family, with the appropriate rewards.

Celebrations of Success Improve Your Relationships. This "reward" phase also may be a good opportunity to improve the relationship tool, by sharing the reward with others that made the achievement of a goal possible, either through direct contribution or moral support. This could include rewarding coworkers, friends, clients, and family members for their help. Keep in mind that if you are a Warrior, chances are you are frequently a little difficult to be around when you are fervently trying to achieve something, and it may be appropriate to periodically reward people for just putting up with you!

But Don't Get Carried Away with the Trappings of Success. Of course, the rewards shouldn't overshadow the accomplishments. I know many Warriors who constantly overextend themselves, living in overpriced houses and driving cars and boats they can't afford, simply because they incorrectly established these "toys" as their reward, often buying them before the reward had really been earned. But these kinds of rewards become short term, because they require constant feeding to maintain.

This "lifestyle feeding" ultimately becomes a burden, distracting Warriors from their core missions, and always presenting the possibility that Warriors will essentially become slaves to these possessions and potentially lose their status as Warriors by resorting to less-than-admirable traits to maintain their lifestyles. Instead, Warriors should seek the peace of stability in certain parts of their lives, to balance their other personality traits that tend to keep them moving all the time.

Include Altruism as One of Your Goals. Some Warriors, blessed with truly selfless hearts, set their goals and rewards based on how they can help others. Warriors in true public service may therefore receive their rewards as a natural extension of achieving their goals. For instance, someone striving to build housing for the homeless gets great satisfaction and his or her reward when the homeless move in.

Don't Lose Perspective on What's Really Important in Life. Without a guidepost and reward tool, it is easy for Warriors to find themselves in a state of constant dissatisfaction without really knowing why. And by honestly assessing progress against a guidepost, it's easier for Warriors to tell if they are properly using their tools.

We've probably all seen examples of Warriors who lived life on a virtual treadmill, working hard and achieving career and/or financial success without any end in sight, or without taking any reward for their efforts. At some point, they lose perspective on their initial dreams and goals. They awake one day to determine that they are simply dissatisfied, that somehow in the midst of all their work and success, they have let their dreams slip away.

For example, when I was growing up, there was a prominent businessman in town who appeared to own half the state. He was constantly expanding his enterprises; building new companies, large real-estate developments, and office buildings. But the joke of the community was that, despite his riches, he lived life almost as a pauper. He lived in a bad part of town in an old run-down house he had inherited from his parents forty years earlier. He drove a twenty-five-year-old car, and he dressed in one of three black suits he had owned for over a decade. Although he was certainly not a miser to others and was generous to charities in town, he seemingly spent nothing on himself and his family.

After he died, his son informed me that during his entire upbringing, they had never taken a family vacation or done anything that capitalized or took advantage of the huge wealth his father endeavored to build. "Dad was never convinced or comfortable with the fact that he was a success, so he just kept going," he told me about his father, "driving himself harder and harder without any real end in sight." It's a sad situation when Warriors put all their tools to best use, and then don't enjoy the fruits of their labors.

#10: THE COMPASSION TOOL

Count your blessings, and thank God everyone isn't a Warrior. We Warriors can be a grumpy and intolerant bunch! It's easy to have the unrealistic expectation that everyone should be as motivated as we are, and given our hefty egos, we can be pretty tough on those around us. But the Warrior should strive for more. Although it's perfectly acceptable, and in fact necessary, to have high expectations of your performance and those you work around, ideally, Warriors create benevolent and peaceful places for their souls to reside. They have to keep in mind that luckily everyone isn't a Warrior; otherwise, society would be an awfully competitive and harried place.

Keep Your Goals in Perspective. Unfortunately, this can be one of the most difficult levels for a Warrior to reach. Part of achieving that goal is understanding that everyone isn't like you (a fact that really works to your advantage). It is also important to put everything into perspective. Warriors get so focused on achieving their goals that they often lose perspective about the overall importance of that achievement in the big scheme of things. Making that big bonus would pale in comparison to a major health problem or the loss of a loved one. Hence, I often meet Warriors who have overcome a serious disease or conquered some other major personal battle that gave them a completely new perspective on life. Warriors understand that, although many people's problems are of their own creation, there are equal amounts that happen through no fault of their own, and Warriors should strive to help, because they may need assistance someday.

Warriors tend to exist in some form in almost every culture, and one of my favorite cultural representations of the Warrior comes from Eastern teachings (though this is a state I am far from achieving). Such Warriors are at peace most of the time and are filled with compassion for the trials and tribulations that people often have no control over. Yet they possess a power that is always present and occasionally rises to the top. They realize that having a Warrior's power is a gift that was granted to them, and that it is also their responsibility to hone and develop the gift and to work with others who have been granted the gift to also develop it to its most positive form. They also have compassion for those who do not have the Warrior's power, and they protect them from the Weasels who would take advantage of them. Although unfortunately, all Warriors do not regard their "gift" in this manner, it is an admirable way for budding Warriors to channel their energies.

. . . .

In the next chapter, we'll take a look at some of the practical applications of the Warrior's tools, including case studies of a few well-known and not-so-well-known Warriors who have particularly excelled.

Warriors in Action (and Missing in Action): How to Use Warrior Tools Effectively

"Success is 1 percent inspiration and 99 percent perspiration."
— Thomas Edison

If your goal is to be a Warrior, by now you've taken an inventory of your own tools, made your first step toward tuning them a bit, and probably have a pretty good feel for the areas in which you are strong— and those that need work. If your inventory didn't fare too well, don't give up, because being a successful Warrior doesn't necessarily mean that you have a completely full box of tools that you skillfully use at all times (although that is usually the mark of the consummate Warrior, and life will be much easier if you move toward this position).

Properly utilizing the toolbox requires some natural ability, discipline, concentration, and practice. Many Warriors operate below their peak, but still quite successfully, by mastering just a few of their own key tools and using them to their best advantage. It is equally important to eliminate the misuse of tools, and to make sure you aren't using Whiner and Weasel crutches.

Let's take a look at a few real-life examples of Warriors and Warriors-in-development, and a few other examples of Warrior wannabes who didn't quite master the use of their tools. They all use their tools to various degrees of success. As you will see, although many Warriors become successful utilizing their Warrior tools, they often don't reach their full potential because during the process, they discard or misuse some of their additional tools.

CASE STUDY #1

A Warrior Who Mastered His "Personal Brand"
(and Quite a Few Other Tools)

One of the most fulfilling and exciting opportunities in my career was to work with television legend Johnny Carson. For the five years leading up to his death, I was proud to be Carson's partner in marketing his video library from his thirty years of hosting *The Tonight Show*. Working in conjunction with Carson and Jeff Sotzing, Carson's nephew and president of Carson Productions, we created and marketed one of the biggest selling video and DVD collections in history that continues to set sales records years after its initial release.

While the opportunity to get to know Carson and work with such incredible material was a great pleasure, one of the most valuable things I derived from the relationship was observing how Carson, the consummate Warrior, utilized his tools. Carson was particularly good at building and maintaining his personal brand, which has become one of the most memorable in entertainment history. And this mastery was never more evident than when he passed away. Despite the fact that he had been retired and had virtually disappeared from public life thirteen years earlier, Carson's death was accorded the massive media coverage and respect normally reserved for presidents and kings. We all remembered the best about Carson, which I suspect was exactly what he would have wanted.

Major celebrities essentially become household brands, but unfortunately when their brands lose their luster and age (as they all ultimately do), most celebrities discard their brand equity, and do anything to stay in the spotlight, often denigrating themselves and destroying their legacy. It is a sad experience to see great actors you once admired relegated to hawking horrible products (though I must admit that in my business I depend on the fact that a few celebrities are willing to take the money and run), or more recently descend into the world of reality shows, where they might consume bugs, move into wacky households with psychos and criminals, or humiliate themselves in some other way just to be on camera.

In contrast, Carson was the master at managing his career with elegance, dignity, and an air of mystery that added to his celebrity allure. Though I never heard Carson specifically address the management of his personal brand, he seemed to intuitively know exactly how to do it better than almost anyone else. A few of Johnny Carson's secrets included:

- *Don't overstay your welcome, and maintain the mystique.* Carson could never understand why so many in the public eye stayed well past their prime. He wanted to be remembered at his best, and consequently though he could have extended his time on television many more years, he went out in his prime. Unlike so many celebrities and wannabes that do anything (even degrade themselves) to stay in the public eye, Carson actually avoided the press at almost any cost. When I started working with him, I was surprised to learn that he never even utilized a publicist. He understood that his reclusive nature made him more interesting to the public, and it also allowed him to maintain his privacy.

- *Carson stayed true to his word.* When Johnny Carson said something, he meant it—so when he said he was retiring, he stayed retired, unlike many celebrities who use retirement and their emergence from retirement as a gimmick to sell themselves. Though he had constant offers to do that "one special appearance" or endorsements for huge sums of money, he stayed true to his word. This was a powerful trait that transferred to those he worked with too, which allowed Carson to better control his personal brand. When working with Carson, we knew it was essential to do exactly as we had promised, and we established a zero tolerance policy for customer service problems that stands to this day.

- *Quality was King for the King of Late Night.* Nobody was more critical of his work than Johnny Carson. With more than 4,500 hours of television spanning thirty years, the television library he built was the largest in television history, featuring some of the greatest stars and moments in TV history. But despite the fact that I constantly advocated releasing more of the library and we could have increased our sales by tens of millions, Carson insisted that only the very best from his career be released to the public.

- *Carson maintained quality control at any price.* Earlier in his career, Johnny Carson experimented with many extensions to the Carson brand. Believe it or not, there were Johnny Carson suits and clothing, Carson cologne, and even Johnny Carson Steakhouses. One day in the 1970s, one of Carson's friends called to let him know he had purchased a Johnny Carson tie, and it had fallen apart. Carson immediately investigated his clothing line and found it to be below his standards. Despite the fact that it was a hot seller and he would lose millions in sales, he pulled it from the market. Soon after that he pulled out of all his other business endeavors and endorsements. He understood that by putting his brand in the hands of others whom he really could not control, he risked everything else he had built.

Carson was a master at using many of his other Warrior tools and seeing him in action made me realize why he has been the consummate talk show host. Johnny Carson understood the essence of communication. A few years ago, as a reward to the team that worked on his video series, Carson invited the group to lunch. Of course, lunch with Johnny Carson was a huge treat for my staff members, and they were all a little wide-eyed as we entered his office. Carson spent a minute or two meeting each of the ten people; learning their names, a little about their job, and background; and generally making them feel comfortable. At lunch he managed to have conversations with almost all of them, commenting on where they were from, and keeping the group entertained. I was most amazed to observe that Carson correctly remembered each person's name throughout the day (like most people, I have trouble retaining one person's name for more than a few minutes—much less ten people), and he engaged them in two-way conversations. While most stars are used to just pontificating about themselves, Johnny Carson was curious about others and really enjoyed the art of conversation. And despite the fact that he became perhaps the biggest television star in history, he managed to keep himself reasonably well grounded.

CASE STUDY #2

A Warrior Who Mastered the "Guidepost and Reward"
(and Many Other Tools)

Before his tragic death, Jay Call was the retired founder and CEO of Flying J, a nationwide chain of companies in the travel services industry. He started the enterprise with a single little gas station in a small town in Utah, and by the time he was fifty years old, he had built a $10 billion enterprise and one of the largest travel services companies in the world. Flying J continues to be the hallmark of industry, and Jay Call's legendary talents and innovation are a tremendous legacy.

Call built a huge cadre of friends and admirers, and his success afforded him all the perks of an enormously successful Warrior. He enjoyed several beautiful homes and estates, a yacht, a fleet of luxury automobiles and motorcycles, and perhaps most important among these possessions to Call, a collection of aircraft. Call is a good example of the proper utilization of a wide range of Warrior's tools.

Putting the Guidepost and Reward Tool Forefront. Flying was Call's great passion in his life, and it motivated him to be successful in his career. Hence, he made it an integral part of his company's development by actually naming the company Flying J. "I kind of tracked my own career success by the kind of planes I could afford to fly," he once told me, starting out with a small single engine Tri-Pacer and finally ending up with a fleet that included two private jets. Call also found a way to utilize his passion to make himself successful in other ways. Integrating doing what you love into your job is often a recipe for success. The fact that he was a pilot made him incredibly mobile. He had a sixth sense for picking locations on which to build his travel plazas, and the fact that he could easily fly himself anywhere he needed to go, and observe traffic patterns from the air helped him pick the right locations.

Develop Your Warrior Tools Early. From the time he was twenty years old and running his first little service station, he was careful to develop his integrity and relationship tools. Older and more successful men in the oil business liked Call and the fact that he always kept his word and seemed to have boundless energy, ideas, enthusiasm, and drive (he mastered the relationship and integrity tools at an early stage).

It's always a good idea for young Warriors to build close relationships with older Warriors and Workers, because they cannot only help you, but they also present major blockades to your success if they feel threatened or competitive. Although most Warriors eventually are forced to "take on the competition" at various points in their careers, they are always well advised to pick their battles carefully. Although Warriors face conflict without hesitation, and often with almost a sense of elation, they should always avoid needless conflict with competitors, because it can tremendously hamper productivity. Experienced Warriors like to control the battle and the battlefield.

Most Warriors I talk to also continually emphasize the importance, if possible, of finding a key mentor in their early development. This stands in stark contrast to Weasels, who usually tend to operate from a feeling of isolation, with few, if any, role models they admire.

Continue to Grow and Work toward Greater Goals. It was this drive (and, of course, a good understanding of the business) that helped Call open several additional gas stations within a few years of starting his first one. He found that he had a much attuned intuition tool that gave him a real knack for choosing good locations, and he had the courage to follow his intuition by continuing to build new stations.

He also extended many aspects of his personal brand into his company. Call was a particularly fastidious and organized man—with an almost "Felix Unger-like" attention to orderliness. He extended his compulsiveness for cleanliness into his gas stations and truck stops (a business where "clean and organized" were adjectives normally not found). He found that road-weary patrons appreciated his attention to detail. He also extended his relationship tool into the workplace. Long before frequent-flyer and frequent-buyer programs were commonplace, Flying J was pioneering the concept with a "frequent- fueler" program that rewarded truck drivers with gifts for their regular patronage. He realized that long-term relationships would be the key to his success.

Make It Happen. One of Call's major career breaks came as a result of his own audaciousness (and use of his make-it-happen tool). After amassing several stations (and a bigger plane to mark his success), he decided that he could greatly increase his profitability if he owned his own refinery (an admirable goal, but normally only one that a considerably larger company would entertain). He identified a chain of service stations and a refinery for sale that were many times larger than his current operation. And despite the fact that he didn't have the credentials, money, or management infrastructure to buy the company, he somehow managed to pull off the deal through a combination of leveraging his current operation, and immediately selling off some of the assets of the company being purchased.

A few years later while on vacation at his home in Palm Springs, he read in the *Wall Street Journal* that a large Canadian-based oil company was for sale, with several major American oil companies in the running to buy it. With a Warrior's confidence, and seemingly unconcerned with the fact that he would be competing with billion-dollar international conglomerates, he jumped in his plane and flew to Canada intending to buy the company. Imagine the reaction of the Canadian oil company executives when he knocked at the door—the owner of a company much smaller than their operation—offering to buy them out.

And that is exactly what he accomplished! He managed to construct a risky and complicated financial deal that allowed him to pay a premium price for the company. Utilizing relationships with some of his old mentors and a history of paying his bills established with lending institutions, he pre-sold parts of the company he didn't need, using the cash to immediately pay down the huge debt he had taken on. Within a few years, he had parlayed the two acquisitions into a strong and growing national chain, and much to his delight, he upgraded to a jet!

Give Credit Where Credit Is Due. Call was always quick to point out that he owes a lot of his success to the other smart people he hired early in his career. This is typical of successful Warriors. They tend to acknowledge their own strengths and weaknesses, and they compensate for their own shortcomings by bolstering their weak areas with talented people. Typically, because Warriors tend to be "dynamic big-picture" people, they depend on key financial types to make sure the detail work gets done. And because many Warriors tend to be overly controlling, it's essential that they allow these key people to do their jobs unhampered once they have proven themselves. Call was fortunate to hire a brilliant financial manager early in the company's development, and he allowed him to do his job unhampered, which was key to his success.

Know What to Look for When Hiring. Call knew that the key to his success was hiring people who shared his drive and goals, and he had some interesting approaches during the interview process. "Whenever I was interviewing someone for a job, I always first looked at their shoes," he laughed. "If they didn't come for a job interview in clean, polished shoes, I knew they would never fit in here. If they passed that test and had all the other required talents, I would walk with them to the parking lot so I could see their car. I didn't care if it was an old or a cheap car, I just wanted to see how they kept it up. Was it clean? Were the windows clean? Or was it full of old hamburger boxes and beer cans? If they didn't keep a clean car, they wouldn't be a good fit for me."

Certainly in today's dynamic business environment, there are a lot of successful Warriors and Workers out there who probably couldn't pass Jay Call's cleanliness test, but it is hard to argue with success. Warriors tend to develop philosophies of business that keep them consistent in their approach, and consistency wins in the long run. And personally, I now find myself paying close attention to a job applicant's shoes.

CASE STUDY #3

It's Never Too Late to Make It as a Warrior

Warriors are not always Warriors from the start. Even if you have slipped into the morass of serious Whiner or Weasel behavior, you can still sometimes find redemption if you activate and properly use your Warrior tools.

Take Dianne, for example. She is the middle-aged president and owner of a successful consulting firm Although business is going well now, things have not always been so rosy.

After graduating from a good university with a master's degree, Dianne bounced around from job to job, finding reasonably good positions but never really working her way up in any organization to the level she desired.

It's Easy to Become a Whiner or a Weasel. By the time she reached her forties, Dianne's inability to succeed past a certain point had begun to take a toll on her, gradually transforming her into a Whiner (with strong Weasel tendencies emerging). Instead of using her tools and accurately assessing her own job performance and worth to the organizations she was being paid by, she instead felt she was a "victim," blaming her inability to rise in her career on office politics and other non-issues. This is a deadly, career-stopping response for Warrior wannabes. Warriors realize that they possess free will, and they constantly utilize their self-responsibility tool. If their careers are not going well, they take responsibility to change the situation in their work environments, or they move on to better situations. They never just stand still and lament their situations or blame others for their plight.

Dianne began to play classic Weasel and Whiner games: refusing to take responsibility and backstabbing supervisors, bosses, and coworkers. She built a personal brand filled with words like "untrustworthy," "gossip monger," and "snake in the grass."

Initially, she had some success with the approach. Unfortunately, Weasel and Whiner crutches can sometimes be used effectively for short periods of time, especially if they are used on other Whiners and Weasels. She managed to convince a competitive company that she was, in fact, the "brains behind her operation," and based on this misrepresentation, she was awarded a major new position that she was completely under-qualified for. Within a year, she had misused her new job. Sensing that the ax was about to fall and smart enough to move on, Dianne quit and announced she was going into business for herself.

Although she did manage to quickly launch her own company, she had not changed her Whiner and Weasel ways. She did have some initial success in attracting clients. But she consistently overpromised and under-delivered. Ultimately, her company failed. Forced to declare bankruptcy, with her personal brand at an all-time low, she took a hard look at her personal and professional life.

"I realized in my heart that I was really best at being a deal maker, and that things fell apart for me after the deal was put together," she explained. "I enjoy the front end of the new business process: identifying clients, the courting process of developing relationships, putting together the deal from the big picture. Once the deal was done, I lost interest."

Find Your True Talent—and Focus on It. Luckily, Dianne discovered that her talent for putting together deals was sorely lacking at—and needed by—many companies. In fact, although there were many fine operations in the industry that could actually do the work, there was a shortage of energetic and talented deal makers who could attract clients and close deals. She began doing independent consulting work, assisting corporations in strategizing and orchestrating new business pitches, and building relationships and joint ventures with other complementary companies. Acting almost like an agent for her clients, she found a market niche that allowed her to work for companies that, in many cases, she used to compete with. And because she only performed the functions in the process she was good at and competent to perform, she built a base of happy clients.

Rebuild Your Personal Brand. Dianne also embarked on the painful process of rebuilding her personal brand, first by doing extensive amounts of volunteer work for industry trade organizations and by speaking at different industry functions. To assist with the dreaded detail work, she found a partner for her business who in many ways was her direct opposite. He countered her flamboyance and big-picture perspective with a more reserved and detail-oriented nature. And she used her aggressive and outgoing personality to build relationships throughout her business. Although Dianne will certainly always enjoy a bit of juicy gossip, she stopped the Whiner and Weasel ways that had hampered her reputation in the past.

In just a few short years, Dianne completely turned her life around. Her consulting business now flourishes, and she is one of the most respected and powerful people in her industry.

Do What You Love to Do. Johnny Carson's, Jay Call's, and ultimately Dianne's stories all share another similarity. They all ultimately found success doing what they loved to do. Though "do what you love, and the money will follow" is an old adage, I found that most happy and well-rounded successful Warriors and Workers truly do love their work and swear by the axiom.

I have certainly found it to be an absolute truth in my own life. Early in my career, I worked in the family business for a few years. Although I had a few talents that brought me a few successes in the industry, I had no passion or love for what I was doing, and I ultimately sought to artificially change my job, which led to near disaster. Transforming a business to better suit your personality, as opposed to finding a business you are suited for, is always a bad idea. Finding business environments I enjoyed immediately made me much more successful.

This seems to be a constant theme in family-owned businesses. I encounter many unhappy second- and third-generation business owners who went into the family enterprise out of a sense of obligation, or to take advantage of the easy advancement, only to find they are miserable in their jobs. They often then become Whiners, or they unwittingly bring down the organization because their heart is in the wrong place.

In the end, this serves no one, because miserable people do not make good business leaders. Businesses and employees deserve happy and energized people at the helm. Often, those who are unhappy with their careers and situations will subconsciously make bad decisions that they know will ultimately force them to make a change. In the meantime, these decisions can lead to the unnecessary destruction of companies and environments.

Don't Set Goals Based Purely on Financial Remuneration. I also consistently meet people unhappy with their careers because they choose a profession based solely on financial potential. Although they might have the accouterments of success, they are unhappy in their lives. This seems especially true in professions normally thought of as "big-money jobs." For instance, a sizable percentage of the attorneys I have had contact with express dissatisfaction with their lives, often saying they were lured into the profession by the image of big money and fancy offices, but that they have no love for the work.[1] But the good news is that there is always

---

1. This also leads to further negative consequences for society, as we have a business environment filled with unhappy individuals taking their frustrations out on society doing the only thing they know how to do—which leads to a system of almost parasitic litigation!

redemption available—even late in life—for those who have gone down the wrong career or life path. It just involves making choices that might seem hard at first but that offer a lifetime of satisfaction.

CASE STUDY #4

A Win/Lose Attitude Is Always a Loss

Ray is an enormously successful Warrior. Over the last twenty-five years, he and his partners have built a product distribution company from a "college kid's start-up" into an almost billion-dollar international enterprise, with more than two thousand employees that dominates its industry. To achieve this success, Ray actually ignored most of his potential tools; instead, he simply concentrated on using the "I'll Make it Happen" tool. He is, without doubt, one of the most aggressive Warriors I have ever met, a human pit bull, continually focused on growing his company, and he is particularly enamored with accumulating more personal wealth. He not only ignores the problems and blockades that would stop most businesspeople in their tracks, but in fact attacks them, in most cases, successfully. "No" does not exist in Ray's vocabulary, nor does he allow anyone in his organization to take no for an answer when it comes to progressing his business.

Don't Ignore the Valuable Relationships You've Established. However, Ray's aggression has taken a toll on his friends and employees, and even on Ray personally. Somehow in the midst of building his company, he completely lost track of his relationship tool, and he adopted a "beat-everyone-into-submission" attitude. Sadly, Ray probably somehow takes pride in this fact, because he regards the success he has achieved as vindication for his bad actions and treatment of people. He is a bully to his staff and suppliers, which causes a tremendous amount of turnover and lack of loyalty. He believes that his company is solely for his benefit, and accordingly he can treat staff and suppliers any way he chooses. In private, his employees and suppliers frequently complain about what a miserable experience it is working for him, which, of course, results in less-than-optimum performance and a real lack of loyalty. They are afraid to make suggestions and innovate, for fear of Ray's irrational temper.

The lowest price does not always make the best deal, and Ray is a good illustration of this fact. He negotiates constantly and brutally, to the point that many good suppliers refuse to do business with him. Others who know him well artificially raise their prices before the negotiations begin, in anticipation of his antics.

He is also well known for his "win/lose" philosophy. He believes that, in any business scenario or negotiation, he must always emerge the clear winner, and the other side, the clear loser. If his suppliers, banks, and other business partners are not unhappy after doing a deal with him, Ray is disgruntled because he feels he did not push hard enough.

Don't Become a Tyrant. There are many successful Warriors like Ray who have lost control of their "I'll Make it Happen" tool, and they live their business and personal lives as virtual tyrants. The problem is that they continue to receive negative reinforcement. Because they are so good with one of their tools, (and usually also because of timing and other innovation issues), their bad treatment of others is rewarded with continued success.

In the end, I would argue that although these individuals may have found a path to success, they never really achieve their true maximum potential because of their misuse of the relationship tool. Ray has certainly built a great business, but think how much better off he would be if he had a staff of people as motivated as he is and eager to achieve more for the company, as opposed to an unhappy group that goes through the workday in fear. Even though his company is successful now, certainly many more potentially lucrative deals would have come to Ray if his personal brand contained words like "nice guy to do a deal with" as opposed to "abusive jerk." Perhaps he would have a two- or three-billion-dollar company, and he would also be able to enjoy the camaraderie of those around him.

Building personal and professional scenarios that offer a win/win for everyone involved is always the best possible solution. Good feelings for both parties are the essence of establishing good long-term relationships, and with good relationships, it is possible to get people to go that extra mile to achieve even more success.

CONCLUSION

Proper personal brand management and establishing motivating rewards can be powerful tools in assisting the Warrior in achieving his or her goals, And as noted in Kevin's and Ray's stories, Warriors are at constant risk of letting their egos and aggression take them to unhealthy and unhappy places. Because Warriors always tend to be in a hurry, they tend to be impatient with others, and they misjudge the effect of this impatience on those around them. They often get unreasonably focused on a goal, and as a consequence, they forget about all the good in their lives and how they are actually progressing against their guidepost and reward tools.

And as their egos grow, it is an easy step to go from self-confident to an insufferable and abusive egomaniac. One of the best ways to stay in check is to periodically assess how you are doing with your relationships, as they are the best method to judge your impact on those around you.

• • • • • • • • • • •

In the next chapter, we'll take a look at a "recipe for failure,"
a serious attitude or condition that frequently stops otherwise talented people
from achieving their goals.

A Recipe for Failure:
Insecurity in Many Forms—and
How to Overcome It

Throughout this book, I have highlighted several personality types that, if left unchecked, can be recipes for failure. These are mind-sets or even physical conditions that can potentially become blockades to happiness, advancement, and productivity, and they can easily lead people down the path to becoming Whiners or Weasels.

In the case studies, drills, and other sections of the book, you will notice that these personality types appear frequently in some form. However, because of their importance, I am choosing to specifically call out a few of them in their own short chapters. Some of these personality types are more severe and deep-seated than others, and it is certainly not my anticipation that after reading a one- or two-page overview, you will immediately begin to drop your negative habits. But perhaps you will recognize some of these traits within yourself and at least begin to make progress toward replacing recipes for failure with a more positive approach.

SEVEN WAYS INSECURITY IS REVEALED

Certainly, the biggest recipe for failure that almost all of us face is insecurity. It can manifest itself in many ways. Although one person's insecurity might force him or her into isolation, or keep that person from pursuing opportunities he or she would be well-suited for, another person might combat his or her insecurity by taking the opposite approach and becoming too verbose, or even a blowhard (as mentioned in chapter 6).

Obviously, to be a Warrior, you ultimately have to conquer your insecurities—or at least learn to manage them. But one of the most disheartening things I have observed watching many friends, family, and employees is the terrible limitations their insecurities place on many of them. These insecurities typically lead to one of the following approaches:

1. Having Extreme Risk Aversion. For some people, even though you might have the talent and the resources to make something happen, your insecurities won't allow you to take even a modicum of risk. You're stuck in one place. Even though you know you could do more, your fear keeps you from trying.

A certain measure of risk is inherent in almost everything that is worth achieving, whether you are managing a financial portfolio, progressing in your career, or even planning a fun night out on the town. Pushing yourself a bit always feels a little risky, but in the end, it can lead to all kinds of rewards.

2. Going into Hiding. We all have coworkers, schoolmates, or even family members who might be around us but are barely noticed. They quietly stay in the background, or they often simply choose not to attend functions that they would enjoy or would otherwise benefit them, just because of their insecurities. While many people just genuinely enjoy their solitude and don't seek attention, I frequently see talented employees fade into the wallpaper and miss opportunities for advancement that they would really like to pursue—just because of their insecurities. If you don't get the promotion, the raise, the date, or some other desired outcome because you were too busy being invisible, it is your own fault.

3. Slipping into the "Big Freeze." I saw this happen just the other day to one of my most talented employees. This employee has progressed tremendously in his career, but from day one, he has suffered from enormous insecurity issues. To his credit, he has been working to conquer the problem, participating in public speaking courses during the evenings to overcome his fear of speaking, and pushing himself in company meetings to make his presence known. However, during a major presentation to clients, he just froze, when he lost his place during a speech. Luckily, other team members jumped in to save the situation.

4. Babbling. I have frequently seen otherwise talented people fall to their insecurities during tense moments in the workplace, and for some reason, they feel a need to fill any silence with often nonsensical chatter. It is better to be silent and look thoughtful than to fill the airwaves with noise.

5. Playing the Passive/Aggressive Game. Insecure people often dance around the real issue and take a convoluted approach toward achieving their goals. Instead of going to the boss and saying, "Here is all the progress I have made this year; here is what I did to improve the company; and accordingly, here is the raise I think I deserve and is justified," they play emotional games or sometimes even have others plead their case. I have had spouses of employees approach me at company parties to tell me their significant other is too shy to ask, but they would really like a raise. I have even had employees get key clients to approach me to proclaim, "He's great—whatever you're paying him is not enough." Although I love the idea that my customers appreciate the staff, and I am especially impressed when the service is so good that clients go out of their way on their own to sing someone's praises, I don't want the staff to use family members or customers to negotiate their raises.

One of my relatives constantly uses a passive/aggressive approach when seeking favors. Instead of coming to me and saying, "I am having a few financial problems and was hoping I could borrow some money. Here is my plan to improve my situation, and here is how I will repay you," she instead says, "Things are pretty bad for me right now. I am broke. Of course, I would never ask you for money, and I am certainly not asking you now, but I just don't know what I'm going to do." Rational people appreciate a direct approach.

6. Adopting a "Tough Guy" Approach. A good friend of mine is a terrific person in a one-on-one situation, but in a business environment, she frequently feels insecure, and she masks these insecurities by being overly tough. Being abrupt or even abusive to people to hide your own feelings of self-doubt is always a bad idea.

7. Overcompensating. Often, the most insecure person in the room is the one with the biggest mouth. To combat their insecurities, many people choose to become overly aggressive—or blowhards who are difficult to trust.

HOW TO OVERCOME THESE FAILURE FACTORS

The good news is that, like almost any other condition, you can overcome your insecurities, if you are committed to do so. This process begins with an honest assessment of your situation and a plan of action to gain the necessary confidence. Do you fit any of the above profiles? I know at some time in my life, I have incorrectly resorted to almost all of the above techniques during times when I was not feeling particularly self-assured. The first step is an honest assessment of your self-image to work through the issues you need to confront. Depending on the depths of your insecurities, there are then a number of more tactical steps you can take to improve your situation.

Increasing communication and confronting your shyness is usually a great first step. I very much appreciate the friend or employee who feels enough confidence to pursue an honest dialogue when necessary. In the business setting, it helps me if I understand my workers' insecurities, so hopefully, through training and perhaps a little ego boosting, we can make improvement.

I also personally find that forcing yourself into a public setting is a great way to gain self-confidence. The "fear of being in the spotlight" tends to be at the root of most people's insecurities, and a good first step is to practice the art of speaking in front of a crowd. Almost every city has a Toastmasters or similar organization that can offer valuable experience. Many social organizations have structures that allow for terrific training by presenting to groups. If progressing in your work environment necessitates making presentations, I would encourage discussing your fears with your boss and asking for opportunities to work through them, perhaps doing presentations to less-intimidating groups of coworkers before working your way up. The only way to conquer your insecurities is to confront them.

And the fact is that you own your insecurities, and it is up to you to learn to deal with them. Unfortunately, it is easy to let insecurities rule your life and then, when you don't achieve your dreams, start whining about injustice.

. . . .

In the next chapter, we perform a little tune-up to your tools.

WARRIORS

CHAPTER 9

A Warrior Drill:
Time to Tune Up Your Tools

"Life consists not in holding good cards but in playing those you hold well."

—Josh Billings

Note: This chapter is an "interactive" section of the book, and you have two choices to fully utilize the questionnaires. Get a pen and paper ready and circle your answers, or go online at www.warriorsandweasels.com. The online version has additional scenarios and features.

So do you possess a Warrior's toolbox? Or perhaps you own a few of the tools listed in chapter 6, but now you really want to fill up your box. Well, this chapter offers a quick drill to assist you in determining which of your tools are fully functional, which ones need a little maintenance, and which tools you don't yet own and need to be added to your collection. Each drill features different work and life scenarios for you to respond to. And as ridiculous as some of the answers may sound, keep in mind that they represent a variety of actual responses from similar real situations.

TUNING YOUR INTEGRITY TOOL

First Scenario: Your immediate supervisor is incompetent, and it is reflecting poorly on you. When you do something right, your supervisor takes all the credit, but when your supervisor does something wrong, the blame is somehow shifted to you or one of your coworkers. To compound the problem, your supervisor and his boss are old friends from another company, so you really have no sympathetic ear to complain to. Although you love your work, you are growing more and more dissatisfied because of the politics of the situations. The following are some possible reactions, with the rationale supporting each. Do you:

1. Quit your job? There is no winning in these kinds of scenarios, and the time and effort you would utilize to stay in the position would be better spent in a new position where there isn't an artificial political ceiling.

2. Go around both your supervisor and his or her boss to the big boss? Tell them what's going on—he or she will probably be pleased to hear it, and you might end up with a promotion.

3. Grin and bear it, and wait until the right opportunity arises? Incompetent people don't stay in a position forever, and you're in a good position when the change occurs.

4. Have a talk with your supervisor, and calmly and logically explain your feelings? If your supervisor doesn't address the issue, go to his or her boss and repeat the process.

5. Grow up and play the political game like a Warrior? The first step is to "gather the dirt" on your supervisor and his boss. Find something to leverage against them. Do they "fool around" during off hours, or perhaps drink a bit? Everybody has a skeleton in his or her closet, and you need to protect yourself by finding it and not being afraid to use it before your supervisor or boss comes after you.

Second Scenario: You are a sales representative for Bulldog Computer Company, a small but growing PC manufacturer. Unexpectedly, you get a call from the U.S. Army, expressing interest in purchasing five thousand of your new Roving Bulldog model laptops. The only problem is they need delivery in four weeks, and under maximum production, your company is only capable of producing three thousand laptops by that deadline.

Getting this order would mean a $25,000 bonus to you, and it would be a major coup for Bulldog Computer, likely catapulting the company to an entirely new level. But you are fearful that there is no way you can deliver in time. The following are possible reactions, with a supporting rationale for each. Do you:

1. Write the order and let the production department worry about it? After all, *selling* is your job, *making* the stuff is theirs.

2. Honestly explain the situation to the client and attempt to get an extension on delivery? If the client can't extend, politely refuse the order. It's better to be upfront about the situation than to make excuses when you can't deliver.

3. Accept the order and do whatever it takes to make sure Bulldog delivers?

4. Raise hell with management? After all, if they want to really make this company a success, it is their job to make sure they can fill the orders you bring in, right? If they can't do their jobs, the very least they should do is to compensate you for the lost commissions you have to forego because of their management problems. And if you don't like what you hear, threaten to go to a competitor with the order.

THE SOLUTIONS: HOW TO HANDLE THESE SCENARIOS—AND HOW NOT TO
First Scenario: The Answer Is #4. The first step is to follow the chain of command and calmly and logically explain your position. Any other approach would put you in dangerous Whiner or Weasel territory. A Weasel's first move in any organization is to spread discontent at all levels and attempt to subvert any established chain of command. When you accept employment in an organization, you also accept the implied agreement to honor the chain of command (at least until you have proven yourself so talented and invaluable that you have the option

to change the organization to your vision to make it more productive—but that is done out in the open).

A situation like this is also a good opportunity for a personal "Whiner check." Most of the Whiners I have encountered certainly don't know they are Whiners, and their first drop into the Whiner's abyss is to identify that their bosses (and perhaps some of their coworkers) are flawed.

If you find yourself constantly surmising that your superiors in the workplace are incompetent, you either work in a dysfunctional company (which may present opportunity or disaster), or you are masking your own inadequacies by whining about others. Step back and realistically assess the situation, and if necessary, discuss your view with a knowledgeable third party who will give you fresh insight from an unbiased perspective. Be open to the fact that perhaps the problems you are whining about are your own.

Although Warriors frequently have trouble with business hierarchies, and they certainly don't have time for needless politics and cronyism that hampers productivity, one of the first assumptions you should make in any organization is that "all is not as it seems" for those in positions of power. You need to resist the natural temptation to assume your boss and most of those above your boss are incompetent idiots who are simply there through some hiring fluke, and that they're out to get you because you represent a threat to them via your talent and ambition. After all, they did have the good sense to hire you. As any experienced manager will tell you, talented individuals make their jobs easier, and managers normally welcome them to their team.

Accordingly, talk to your supervisor with an open mind. Explain your perspective on the situation, and in most cases, you will find a receptive ear if you handle the situation properly. If that doesn't work, and you truly feel that a conspiracy of incompetence exists, work your way up the ladder with your complaints, and make sure your position is well documented and supported. You'll have the satisfaction that you followed the chain of command, just as you would want one of your employees to do.

If your suspicions prove to be correct, and upper management is truly corrupt and/or incompetent, there is a good chance that one of the following will occur:

- Thanks to your honesty and dedication, you'll be in line for a promotion.

- You will discover that the company truly is a worthless pit of cronies, incompetents, and Weasels, and that you need to move on.

Second Scenario: The Answer Is #3. The first issue to accept is that you are part of a team, so #1 (laying the problem off on the production department) and #4 (laying it off on management) are options to immediately discard. Write the order and do whatever it takes to make sure your company delivers. Of course, you are going out on a limb a bit with this one, but Warriors take risks—that's why they are Warriors! Every Warrior relates stories of "going for it," when they took the risk of tackling something that at first blush didn't look like it could be done, but by achieving it, they elevated themselves professionally and emotionally for the next Warrior's challenge.

Now I know that in chapter 6, "The Warrior's Toolbox," I discussed that when using the integrity tool it was important not to overpromise, but in this scenario, your challenge is to get your company to overproduce—to achieve something it doesn't think it's capable of. Of course, do whatever you can to set more reasonable expectations from your client. Explain the difficulties, and do whatever you can to negotiate an extension, but in the end, write the order and take it back to your company. Naturally, if it is just physically impossible to deliver, you would not want to make the commitment, but in this case, you need to boost productivity by 25 percent, a task that would seem within the realm of possibility. As a Warrior, for your benefit and the benefit of everyone involved, you need to help your company achieve this difficult but important task, and you'll emerge a leader who helps everyone achieve new heights.

* * * * * * * * * * * *

In the next chapter, we will begin an exploration of the backbone of every operation: the Worker.

PART THREE

Workers—
The Backbone of the Workplace

CHAPTER 10

Seven Types of Workers: Understanding Their Different Motivations

---

"By working faithfully eight hours a day, you may eventually get to be the boss and work twelve hours a day."
—Robert Frost

T he Worker is the foundation of almost everything that surrounds us. The car in your driveway, the house you live in, the food in your refrigerator, and in fact, the refrigerator, are available to you because a cadre of dedicated Workers created them. Warriors might have invented the products, developed the business plans, and financed and started the companies that made the products, but ultimately, Workers manufactured and delivered the finished goods. And to a great extent, these Workers also create the markets that primarily buy the goods and feed the overall economy, making the Warrior's lifestyle possible.

Now, I don't mean to turn this chapter into something that sounds like a 1950s Union-hall meeting, and there is certainly a big difference between someone who simply goes to work and a true Worker, but as mentioned, we would all be in trouble if the majority of the population didn't gladly fit into this category.

I also suspect that if one were to analyze the Four W's to determine the "happiness and satisfaction percentage" of each group, the Worker would rank at the top, ultimately on average happier and more content than even the Warrior. A successful Worker tends to exist in a more simplistic and easier-to-understand social environment, with clearer and more achievable reward and guidepost tools. In contrast, the Warrior (and for that matter Whiners and Weasels) often just feel driven, frequently incapable of any sense of long-term satisfaction, because their goals are constantly shifting.

Growing up in Montana, I was surrounded with a community primarily comprised of happy Workers. Most of the people I knew certainly took pride in their work, but they also lived a balanced existence, with reward and guidepost tools that included achieving their professional goals while balancing family and lifestyle issues. Although they were hard workers and did the best job possible during their eight-hour workdays, they put equal effort into finding happiness and balance at home, in their friendships, and in their leisure activities.

Sometimes, they could be Workers in the workplace and Warriors when it came to their families or other passions. They also tended to take their hobbies quite seriously, sometimes even slowing down commerce for the opening of hunting season or some other activity that enjoyed tremendous appeal throughout the community. This "heartland attitude" is typical of the successful middle-to-upper-middle-class of America. It also tends to slow down the pace of life, as it necessitates making the time and emotional investment to build the family unit and friendships.

Although making enough money is always important, it is not "the most important thing" in these types of communities. And in these communities, those who have achieved big financial success tend to be much lower key about it, because showy wealth is looked down upon. The financial goal tends to be centered around stability—first achieving security via sufficient savings, owning one's own house, etc., and then layering on some of the toys (boats, weekend homes).

These attitudes, if managed properly to maximize productivity, can be quite healthy for a company if there is a Warrior or Warriors in the mix to add the necessary aggression needed to maintain growth and innovation. People tend to "job hop" much less, so there is a core of trained people who understand the business. They take pride in years spent with a company, and they are not as susceptible to outside employment offers that would cause friction in the workplace.

Of course, this is in tremendous contrast to the environment one tends to find in the major cities. When I first started doing business in Los Angeles, I was especially struck by how much the social environment really resembles the cliché jokes that are made about it. The entertainment industry has had a negative impact on Workers in Southern California. There is little value placed on stability and relationships. Instead, people are driven by a celluloid version of life, where success is judged by the ability to attain the right car or a low body-fat ratio. It is an environment in which Warriors thrive, because everyone is always looking to do a deal, but it is problematic for Workers, because it tends to emphasize all the wrong motivations. It also creates financial instability for everyone, as people acquire unmanageable debt levels just to own the toys that give them the appearance of success.

The proliferation of mass media has spread this attitude past the California borders, making the plight of the Worker more difficult over the past few decades. We are bombarded with messages telling us that being a Worker is simply not enough. People certainly find it more entertaining to watch stories about lifestyle extremes. Our television series and movies tend to be about Warriors and Weasels who live the high life, existing in a state of constant dramatic tension that seldom exists in real life (or at least outside of the entertainment industry) or stories of failed Workers living in poverty or crime. Game shows espouse the potential of a lottery lifestyle.

Although there are exceptions, this stands in stark contrast to the way the life of the Worker used to be celebrated twenty or thirty years ago. The "everyday hero Workers" portrayed by actors such as Jimmy Stewart, Spencer Tracy, Henry Fonda, Robert Young, and many others have been replaced by a cadre of action heroes, wealthy Weasels, pontificating trailer trash accusing their relatives of stealing their lovers and spouses, and other less-than-realistic portrayals. So part of my message is "Workers rejoice." Assuming you have found overall satisfaction, and you continue to challenge yourself to fulfill your reward and guidepost tools, you are potentially far ahead of most of the rest of the population.

If you are a Worker reading this who does not feel satisfaction, it is important for you to also do a "reality check" during the next couple of chapters, to make sure you really are a Worker, or a Worker preparing to make the jump to be a Warrior, and not actually a Whiner or Weasel. Being on the cusp of the negative side prevents you from being the best you can be in your position. And if you are on the cusp of becoming a Warrior, these chapters should help you achieve your goals.

WORKERS WORK IN ALL PROFESSIONS AND ALL JOB LEVELS

You will find Workers in virtually every profession and at every social stature. The Workers I discuss in the Four W's are not synonymous with the "blue-collar worker" we normally think of when the term "worker" is used. Being a Worker doesn't mean you aren't enormously financially successful, professional, or educated—in fact, it is often quite the opposite. The Worker in the Four W's is simply the stable force in a work or home environment, a member of the support team that delivers on the Warrior's promises. They operate from different motivations than any of the other Four W's, and they usually have a different philosophy about their work and lives. They typically lead a more balanced existence that might be devoid of the tremendous highs a Warrior achieves, but they also avoid the tremendous lows.

Workers are sometimes more successful in their careers than Warriors because they tend to take fewer risks, and if they do end up in the right position, they are often rewarded well. For example, I know brilliant Worker attorneys who have built great practices as the backbones of their firms. They might not be the Warrior rainmakers that bring in the clients, but they put in sixty- and seventy-hour weeks to ensure that their firms keep their clients. There are thousands of successful Worker engineers, architects, doctors, professors, and small business owners. The computer and dot-com revolution has created a boom for the digitally minded Worker. Individuals who just a few years ago would have been relegated to low-paying jobs in graphic design, accounting, and engineering firms now find their skill sets in tremendous demand, placing them at the highest ends of the pay scale. There are similar examples in most industries.

If you are a Warrior, the most important component to assist you in achieving your goals will most likely be a dedicated team of Workers to back you up, and accordingly, it is crucial that you take steps to foster your team and understand the mind-set of a Worker. If you are a Worker seeking to maximize your career potential, it is always a good idea to align yourself with successful Warriors, because they most likely provide easy channels of advancement for you. Warriors tend to build relationships with key Workers that transcend a single job position.

In fact, almost half of the management team in my current company has worked for me at some time previously. A few years ago, I acquired a company based on the fact that I had worked with many of the key staff almost twenty years ago and still remembered how talented they were! During my career, I have been fortunate enough to build a key team of Workers and Worker/Warriors-on-the-cusp that allow me to function properly. Because I have the backing to deliver on the promises I make to clients, business partners, and investors, I can utilize my Warrior tools properly without the fear I will under-deliver.

As covered above, Workers tend to seek some level of stability and balance in their workplace. They often have the interest or ability to focus on certain duties that would drive a Warrior crazy. Workers and many Warriors also tend to fall into several of what I call *motivational categories*. Certainly, all Workers have a core set of requirements: a good work environment and compensation, basic input for the ego, the tools to do their job well, job security, and other normal needs. And the Warrior and/or manager needs to always strive to make sure these basic Worker needs are met. But those issues aside, a happy and productive workforce is built by comprehending the more fundamental and often unspoken motivations (the *motivational categories*) of different kinds of Workers. Warriors and managers need to understand these motivational categories and needs to create and motivate the most effective teams, and Workers should find it valuable to analyze their own motivational categories to make sure they are being fulfilled.

Keep in mind that your supervisor at work, or your family and friends may not be readily cognizant of your motivational categories and the feedback to these categories that you may require to feel fulfilled. Hence, if you feel you are not getting enough feedback to be motivated properly, you may need to better communicate your needs. In fact, it is important to always keep in mind that it is always *your responsibility to communicate your needs and goals to others.*

There is nothing wrong with explaining to others that you are a "Craftsman" or that you fall into one of the other categories detailed in this chapter. I can guarantee you that a good manager, friend, or family member always wants to better understand how to make others feel better. Often, Workers remain silent about these issues, and they tend to just feel unfulfilled, expecting others to innately understand their needs. If it is difficult for you to communicate, feel free to bookmark these pages and highlight one of the sections in this chapter, then give this book to your supervisor, friend, or family member, with a note that says, "I feel this way: this describes me." By understanding and fulfilling these motivational categories, everyone wins.

The rest of this chapter describes the most common motivational categories of Workers.

1. THE CRAFTSMAN WORKER

These Workers tend to derive enormous satisfaction from the quality of the product they create or service they provide, regardless of the type of product they are producing. From a consumer's perspective, working with a Craftsman Worker is usually a great experience, although it can occasionally be frustrating, because a Craftsman can be slow to deliver and sometime difficult to work with on a personal basis.

Although there are certainly many good examples of Warriors and entrepreneurs who exhibit Craftsman tendencies, by and large, Craftsman Worker types are often not well suited to run their own businesses, unless they are in industries that tolerate and compensate accordingly for their attention to detail. For example, I have a friend who is a wonderful woodworker, but unfortunately, he has gone bankrupt in his last two attempts to act as an entrepreneur and manage his own woodworking shop. Left to his own designs, he consistently produces work that is better than consumers are willing to pay for, and so he almost always loses money on his projects. He needs to work in a structured environment with an outside supervisor making the qualitative judgments about what he can deliver for a price consumers are willing to pay, or market his work to a high-end demographic that will appreciate his craftsmanship and allow him to operate at a profitable level. But this also means he has to choose his place of employment carefully, because he also needs to make sure that his employer produces a product of sufficient quality to fulfill his personal need to remain a craftsman.

Craftsmanship can extend to almost any profession. Another of my good friends moved to Portland a few years ago after running an expensive and traditional Italian restaurant in Los Angeles for more than ten years. My friend is a classic craftsman when it comes to food, and more specifically Italian food. From his perspective, every meal should be an experience that one savors. Dinner should last for hours, a celebration of not only food, but also fellowship and the dining experience. He constantly laments the proliferation of chain restaurant-type dining experiences as an assault on modern culture. So of course, when he opened his new restaurant in Portland, it only featured the best quality ingredients, preparations, and wines—with equally attentive tuxedo-clad service.

Unfortunately, after a year of losing money, my friend found that unlike L.A., there was not a large enough market that would make the financial and time investment to appreciate and support his craft. His restaurant failed. This is a common situation in the volatile world of restaurants, and I suspect that a "middleman" who could have balanced Pasqualli's craft with the real market conditions would have been well advised. Unfortunately, the Craftsman is often blinded from real market conditions by his or her love of craft.

Certainly, you will find Craftsmen in all kinds of endeavors, including the manufacturing sector, ranging from the furniture maker to the line worker at an automotive plant who simply takes great pride in hanging a car door properly. Craftsmen also exist in the more highly paid and cerebral professions. I know many Craftsman Worker attorneys, journalists, and teachers who are driven to be the very best at what they do. I recently met a Craftsman physician who had left the traditional medical world to pursue a much less lucrative but much more fulfilling alternative medical practice that allowed him to spend a lot more time with his patients. He didn't feel he could fulfill his role of healer with the assembly-line approach of the regular doctor's office, and he felt that in order to be a craftsman at his trade, he needed to spend more time with his patients and concentrate on really understanding and healing the root of their problems, as opposed to simply prescribing treatments for the symptoms of their illnesses.

In the advertising industry, I work with Craftsmen on a daily basis, from the cameraman who lights the shot "just right" and the makeup person who takes great pride in making people look perfect, to the art director who works late into the night making sure that the ad fulfills his or her vision, which often exceeds even what the client is expecting. Many of the Workers I know in the more traditional trades are Craftsmen, even though one might not initially regard their professions as an art. I have a good friend who paints cars for a living, but to hear him describe his projects and his concern for detail, you would think you were hearing Renoir describe a new painting.

I've met many Craftsman accountants, bartenders, and security guards. Another of my friends is an electrician, but he simply doesn't install wiring; instead, he creates wonderful electrically powered environments for his customers. Many homemakers are true Craftsmen, running their homes efficiently and with style. Even Mark, the parking lot manager where I park my car, is a Craftsman Worker. He takes great pride in the fact that he runs an efficient lot with minimal "door dings," provides an extraordinarily friendly and customer service-oriented environment for his clients, and accordingly, has many happy patrons.

From a manager's perspective, the Craftsman Worker can be a terrific worker to have around, because the quality of his or her finished products is typically topnotch. And in fact, many businesses absolutely need Craftsman Workers as opposed to any other type of Worker. To keep Craftsmen satisfied, a manager must understand their motivational requirements. It is simply not enough to compensate and treat them well. The manager needs to allow them the opportunity to practice their art. That can be as simple as making sure they get more challenging projects to tackle, to providing a few extra needed "tools of the trade."

For example, I recently hired a new employee to join one of my companies. He had spent the last twelve years working for a competitor. The competitor was a division of a much larger and more secure parent corporation, and I was unable to offer him a compensation or benefit package that was much better than he was already receiving. However, he jumped ship not because of compensation or any real dissatisfaction with his former employer, but primarily because his previous employer wouldn't purchase a few new tools he felt he needed to do his job to the standards he wanted to achieve.

Not realizing money wasn't the issue, his former employer offered him a raise to stay. For less than the cost of the raise, his employer could have purchased the tools that would have kept him a happy Worker, which ultimately would have resulted in a better product, but the employer did not understand what motivated him. I provided the tools to do his job better, plus a little time away from the job to attend a few seminars to learn how to properly use those tools.

Craftsmen typically have justifiably big egos about the quality of their work (although these egos might not be readily apparent), so their manager needs to give them periodic *ego infusions* (the ego infusion is an important technique). It's essential to see the work through their eyes—to analyze the thought, creative process, and labor-hours that went into a project—and to praise them accordingly. Just because you might not see the artistic integrity of a well-thought-out report, or the way a tree was planted in your front yard, you do need to appreciate the fact that the person who created it might regard it as his or her creative and very personal outlet. By acknowledging the talent and expertise that went into this outlet, you give affirmation to the Craftsman, which is much more important to him or her than money.

But the Craftsman is not always the ideal kind of person for every operation. As appealing as the idea is of someone who regards his or her job as art, it is not always the most efficient and cost-effective approach to business. Sometimes, they are quite specific about what they are willing and unwilling to do, which often makes them a difficult kind of employee for a small company, where everyone needs to do a bit of everything. And even if you do require Craftsmen to fulfill your business requirements, you need to make sure their artistic vision matches yours.

I experienced this firsthand a few years ago while I was running another advertising agency. Although our clients required creative work, they had very specific financial objectives about how their advertising needed to perform. Unfortunately, many of our creative and production staff were totally unconcerned with these issues. They were solely motivated by the ability of their job to allow them total creative freedom, regardless of whether it was right for the client or fell within a reasonable budget. There are certainly advertising agencies that focus on delivering that kind of hyper-creative work, but we were not one of them, and this clash in attitude versus client needs created a lot of turmoil and severely impacted our income statement.

Perhaps the most graphic way to represent this is to once again consider the restaurant. It is possible to purchase a filling and nutritious meal for as little as $3 or $4, or one can pay as much as $100 or more. Naturally, you would never think about putting the chef who prepares the $100 meal to work in an inexpensive diner. He or she would undoubtedly be miserable and most likely either be bad at the job—or would overproduce given the price and margin. Yet in many companies, this commonly occurs. Managers need to understand the mind-set and motivations of their Workers.

If the job is essentially volume- or production-oriented, giving Craftsman Workers little control over what they deliver eventually results in unhappy Workers—or even transforms them into Whiners. Craftsmen in these kinds of situations can also abnormally slow down the process, perhaps even making it unprofitable.

It is a manager's responsibility to analyze the company's business objectives to determine if the Craftsman's approach to detail and quality is justified by the position, and also whether the required work can fulfill the motivational needs of a Craftsman Worker. Often, it is just a matter of putting the right people in the right positions to achieve the best balance for all concerned. Most operations, regardless of the product or service they provide, have room for at least one Craftsman to enhance their offering and motivate other Workers to constantly strive to improve.

And it is the Craftsman's responsibility to realistically assess the requirements of his or her position, to determine whether or not the demands will fulfill his or her personal requirements for happiness.

2. THE PRODUCTION WORKER

As strange as it may sound, luckily for many industries, there are also Workers completely motivated by the completion of a project, as opposed to simply delivering the highest quality. This is not to say that Production Workers do bad work. But they find their motivation via the act of *completion*: finishing a construction project, building a road on schedule, finishing an audit, accomplishing the task at hand on time and on budget. Production Workers normally work in black-and-white environments: give them the goal and timeline, and simply let them go complete the project. And they are best motivated by clear feedback on their achievement of those goals.

From a manager's perspective, they are relatively easy to manage. It is easy to put together compensation and bonus programs based on the completion of an established goal. And communicating and motivating the Production Worker is usually the simplest of all the motivational categories. In most cases, a progress chart with clearly defined goals and bonus thresholds for beating production estimates is all that is required.

This mentality can extend to many different professions. I have had salespeople work for me who were Production Workers. They functioned most effectively with a clear sales quota they had to achieve. But unlike a Warrior who would see the quota as a starting point and would endeavor to set new sales records at any cost, Production Worker salespeople simply seek to achieve the goal you establish, make the amount of money they require, and maintain their free time for their other interests.

Obviously, a manager needs to be careful not to put a Production Worker in a position that requires a Craftsman, and vice versa. Also, Production Workers tend to work better in the background, because customers often prefer the illusion of the Craftsman doing their work, as opposed to a clear "finish-the-project" mentality (although ultimately, they very much appreciate getting the project done).

The key to managing Production Workers is to understand their mindset and to place clear goals and measurement tools in front of them. Without a clear goal and method to track their progress toward achieving the goal, Production Workers often tend to perform at low levels. Their motivation comes through clearly understanding what is expected of them.

3. THE JOB TITLE WORKER

There are a fairly substantial number of Workers who are motivated primarily by job title and the related minor perks (such as management access), as opposed to financial gain or job-satisfaction issues. This can often make for an easy-to-handle motivational category. I have had employees who were willing to forego all kinds of other benefits for the simple joy of having a "Department Manager" or "VP" title on their cards.

But this type of motivation also has to be dealt with judiciously, because frequently being solely motivated by title makes for a bad manager if this Worker type is promoted to a position of power over other employees. Over the years, I have sometimes made the mistake of promoting someone too early because of his or her good work, and the result can be a bit disastrous. I have personally suffered consequences of elevating Title Workers too early without giving them the proper management tools.

For example, Sasha had been one of the best Workers in her department, and when I asked her about what would motivate her to keep expanding her talents in her job, she was focused on becoming a department manager, a position I eventually gave her. However, although she was great as a worker, Sasha was ill-equipped to manage others. She believed in the "manager-as-dictator" approach, setting unreasonably stern rules and procedures for her staff. Morale quickly took a dive, good people quit—and soon Sasha had to be replaced, because the idea of being demoted was too painful for her to accept. By promoting the wrong person and not training her to manage, I lost many good Workers.

Accordingly, when I structure an organization now, I tend to establish few titles, because by nature, they create a level of middle management that can be unproductive, and it also makes the titles that do exist in the company more valued. Titles should be used to establish a reporting flow and give clarity to the organization. Although it is important to give people titles that best facilitates their work and maximizes their odds of achieving their goals, many organizations simply over-use titles. Go into any bank, and almost everyone outside of the teller window will have a "Vice President" attached to their names.

Good Title Workers should have other motivations and satisfactions from their position, in order to be a good leader. They also need to manage by being cognizant of the motivational categories of the people who now fall under their charge. Although it is tempting to often just give people a title when they have performed well at their assigned tasks, a good manager needs to also prepare them for the *responsibilities* of that title; otherwise, you risk negating the value of the title, or upsetting other Workers with an ill-prepared or incompetent manager.

4. THE PROTÉGÉE WORKER

This is one of the best categories of Workers to develop from a management perspective. Protégée Workers are normally Worker/Warriors-on-the-cusp who are seeking Warrior mentors to help them develop into Warriors, or they are simply Workers who derive great satisfaction from their place "on the team." Both types of Protégée Workers need to be managed somewhat differently.

Protégée Warriors-on-the cusp are seeking education, guidance, and feedback that will assist them in their development. From the Warrior or manager's perspective, an assessment needs to be made of them to determine if the investment of time necessary to mentor and keep them motivated is available and justified. Some organizations simply do not have the resources or available openings to develop individuals like this. But assuming they do, the Warrior or manager will discover that this type of Worker will be one of their most dedicated, motivated, hardest-working "workers."

Workers in this category are typically "short term," however, because they fully plan to utilize their positions to hone their Warrior skills and move up the job ladder. Managers need to be aware of this and give them the opportunity to advance at the proper time; otherwise, you risk losing them to a competitor, or worse, having them transform into a Whiner (or even a Weasel), because they may begin to experience frustration at their lack of advancement.

Luckily, Protégée Workers are not always intent on becoming Warriors; otherwise, we would be without a terrific classification of Workers. Many Protégées simply prefer to serve an individual or small group, as opposed to being motivated by the accomplishments of a large organization. They tend to be community oriented as opposed to global in perspective, and they are usually the most nurturing types of individuals to work around. They derive much of their motivation and satisfaction by being a valued assistant or member of a small team. They typically have great appreciation for the talents of their coworkers, and they prefer to regard their workplace almost like an extended family. They potentially work in almost any job, but they seem to thrive in assistant and support service positions, as team players. They are usually there when you need them, happy to put in the long hours necessary to get the job done.

Because they are so agreeable to work around, the manager needs to be careful not to forget about fulfilling the needs of the Protégée Worker. Kind words and compliments go a long way, and because Protégée Workers are typically not clamoring for attention the way other Workers might, a manager needs to periodically give them an ego infusion and make sure their compensation stays in line with their duties and performance. Because they are usually part of a team, the manager needs to allow Protégée Workers to share in the credit for team achievements, even if they were very much "in the back office." A kind word or a pat on the back for a job well done goes a long way with this personality type. This type of Worker also tends not to complain, but if neglected, Protégée Workers will eventually move on or sometimes be transformed into Whiners.

5. THE TEAM WORKER

Many Workers derive their greatest satisfaction from being a key member of a team. Team Workers are often a wonderful addition to a workplace, because they derive their satisfaction from the achievement of overall group or organizational goals, which often tend to be more aligned with the organization's needs than personal goals. It is also usually fairly simple to establish and track group goals and benchmarks, as opposed to the more varied individual goals.

Many businesses would also be enhanced with an infusion of some level of shared group goals into the organization to get the operation running more efficiently together, but this is somewhat dependent on the type of organization. In an operation that is highly dependent on cooperation between employees and departments, it is often advisable to establish incentive programs that reward group cooperation and success.

But sometimes this can backfire, because not all organizations thrive on interdependency. Several years ago, I had a highly ineffective manager working for me who used the "team concept" as a mask to hide his own and other individuals' lack of performance. Although I had encouraged him to set incentive and bonus programs for Workers in his department based on their ability to hit certain performance targets, he fought the idea, explaining that it was more important that his department "work together" and not be torn apart by internal rivalries.

I allowed him to pursue this type of group motivational strategy, only to discover after a year that his department was overstaffed and unproductive, because individuals were not held accountable for their own performance. Certainly, one should analyze how to motivate Team Workers, and they can be wonderful in the right environment, but they are often not well suited for organizations that emphasize individual achievement.

6. THE "SHOW-ME-THE-MONEY" WORKER

Of course, most of us are ultimately motivated by money and cash-based benefits. We want as much as possible, as quickly as possible. It is human nature, and in its purest form, it is really the heart of capitalism, so in some sense it should be embraced.

I have had many wonderful "Show-Me-the-Money" Workers. Our contract was based on the fact that I expected them to make the company a lot of money, and accordingly, they would share some reasonable percentage of the proceeds. And the truth is, I personally like having a lot of these kinds of Workers in my organization. Their motivations are simple to understand. I personally love to make money, and becoming wealthier is high among my guidepost and reward tools.

But unfortunately, most managers are not effective at managing these kinds of Workers, and many "Show-Me-the-Money" Workers are not particularly realistic at addressing their worth to the organization. I am almost constantly faced with Workers requesting extremely high salary and benefit packages that have little correlation to the value of their work. If is frustrating to explain to valued Workers that even though they are doing a wonderful job, their positions could not possibly support their desired salaries. There are financial realities to every position that a profitable operation must respect.

Of course, on the other side of the coin there are the true "Show-Me-the-Money" performers—Workers (and often Warriors) who are at the heart of an organization's profit and success. They should be highly rewarded, and this is where I have seen many managers make their biggest mistake. They make promises or set early large compensation bases for these kinds of Workers, and when the Workers achieve the goals and start to make the big money, they quickly reduce compensation—sort of "anti-motivation." An effective manager needs to develop compensation programs that are motivational and work within the profitability picture of the operation. Then they need to stick to them—even in the face of enormous success by their Workers.

Certainly, a well-rounded worker should not be totally fixated on "Show Me the Money," and through experience, I have learned that Workers who are totally focused on their cash compensation are typically short term in nature and often bad for an organization. However, some degree of financial motivation is as healthy for Workers as it is for the company.

7. THE LIFESTYLE WORKER

The Lifestyle Worker enjoys what many would consider the healthiest approach to work (although others would consider it more European than American). Simply put, their work, although important, takes a backseat to other lifestyle issues, including their family, hobbies, travel, and other outside interests. Work is a means to support the many other more important parts of their lives, and although they might enjoy working, it will always be more of a sideline to their lives.

On the surface, this might sound problematic for the manager, because often Lifestyle Workers are enormously talented, and management would love to have them more involved and dedicated to their jobs. But the key is in using Lifestyle Workers properly, realizing their maximum benefit, while remaining cognizant and living within the limitations of this type of Worker.

Often, they can provide enormous value for the investment. I have had tremendously talented individuals work for me in the past who normally would have been too expensive to hire, but they took lower salary and benefit packages in exchange for reduced responsibilities that allowed them to fulfill their other interests. Often, Lifestyle Workers are actually "retired Warriors" who are seeking a more peaceful environment.

Take Paul, for instance. Paul had an MBA from one of America's top universities. He had achieved early success as a high-level corporate finance executive and entrepreneur. However, when we found him, he was looking for a more laid-back lifestyle that would allow him time to spend with his family and also to manage some of his personal investments. He assumed a CFO position at one of my companies during its infancy at a low salary, when we could not possibly afford someone of his background and qualifications, with the understanding that he would work only three days a week, and that when the company exceeded a certain level in annual sales, he would resign his position. With genuine concern for the company as well as his own desires, he determined at that point we would need a more dedicated person in the position, and we would be able to afford it. True to his promise and talents, in a few short years, he helped steward the company past the annual dollar mark, and he happily passed on the reins to a full-time CFO.

We tried to talk Paul out of leaving, and instead offered a greatly increased salary to jump on the corporate bandwagon. However, in retrospect, this was probably not the best thing to do. Instead of trying to convert Lifestyle Workers who are suited for your organization back into Warriors or attempt to get them to alter their priorities, it is better to design a work plan that suits both of you. Motivate them in ways that really work. For instance, a Lifestyle Worker might prefer a "family-friendly" workplace to more money, or a company-sponsored weekend at a resort may be much more motivational than a more expensive cash bonus. Of course, as with all these motivational considerations, it is not advisable to totally transform your organization to meet all the motivational needs of a wide variety of Workers, but often, even small changes can result in great increases in productivity, without major investment.

Monte was another Lifestyle Worker whom I employed in a sales position—but he had slightly different lifestyle motivations. He loved being on the road. For some reason, he also preferred a spartan approach to traveling, choosing budget motels (sometimes even sleeping in his truck) and hamburger dinners over the nicer travel lifestyle I was willing to provide. However, he was at heart a true outdoorsman, and in exchange for his good work, devotion to the road, and inexpensive habits, he wanted to work a region that allowed him the opportunity to hunt and fish in the evening. He also asked for an extra two weeks off per year (without pay), in addition to his normal vacation schedule, which would allow him a yearly wilderness adventure to Alaska. Luckily, the situation allowed me to grant all these requests, and in return, I received topnotch performance.

Of course, all this assumes that the Lifestyle Worker has a place in the operation. Sometimes their 9-to-5 attitude is simply unworkable in a fast-paced business environment, and it can result in resentment from the other harder-working employees. It is the manager's responsibility to determine the motivational category of a Worker, and best design the operation for efficiency.

CONCLUSION

There are probably dozens if not hundreds of motivational and lifestyle issues that impact the different Workers' attitudes toward their performance and their jobs, but understanding the motivational categories just described will help the Worker and manager in most situations. And although many misinformed managers may argue that Workers are primarily financially motivated and will only respond to money, I would argue that these types of individuals are not really Workers but most likely Whiners or Weasels-on-the-cusp.

The Manager's Responsibility to the Worker. Warriors who are building a team, or managers who are trying to build an effective workplace, need to foster their important and valuable Workers by understanding their motivations and desires. This is sometimes especially difficult for Warrior managers, because they tend to expect that everyone they work with is as driven and responsive to a challenge as they are. This can result in unreasonable expectations about their Workers' performance, which can easily be misunderstood by the Worker as arrogance on the part of the Warrior, or lack of concern. In either case, minor misunderstandings between Warriors, management, and the Workers can make an otherwise terrific workforce unproductive and uncomfortable. Managers need to fill positions with Workers who they can properly motivate within the constraints of the organization, and motivation should be a continuous force.

The Worker's Responsibility to the Manager and Workplace. It is also the Worker's responsibility to understand his or her own motivations and to communicate properly with management. I have had many employees through the years complain that they weren't happy in their positions, but they were unable to tell me why. Management can't read minds.

Ideally, a thriving organization is led by a Warrior or Warriors who set direction for the company and have a dedicated team of Workers who can fulfill the promise. But the key to achieving this is to make sure everyone understands their own motivations—and has the capacity to fulfill them.

• • • • • • • • • • • •

In the next chapter, we will begin our exploration of the less productive and noisier side of the workplace as we dive into the world of Whiners.

PART FOUR

Whiners—And What to Do About Them

CHAPTER 11

"Excuse Me While I Whine": Types of Whiners in Life and the Workplace

"He that is good for making excuses is seldom good for anything else."
—Benjamin Franklin

I hope you will forgive me for climbing on my less-than-lofty pulpit for a few introductory pages in this chapter—to whine about whiners. One of the advantages of writing your own book is that it allows you the opportunity to pontificate freely and without interruption. Please be assured that my less-than-charitable complaints on complaining are not based in any particular political or social ideology, because I have little interest in politicians or politics, and my primary ideology is almost completely reflected in these pages.

WHINERS AREN'T PEOPLE WITH REAL PROBLEMS

My comments to "toughen up" are not directed at those who truly have reason to whine. I think if I were confined to a wheelchair, born lacking limbs, mowed down by a drunk driver, a victim of continual illness, or struck with any of the thousands of other conditions or situations that unfairly and randomly befall people for no good reason, I might be a bit embittered and most likely whiny. Although I pray I would deal with my situation with elegance and optimism for the future, I certainly hope I never have to find out. The many heroes who endure these kinds of pain and problems and who manage to stay cheery and productive deserve a lot of credit, because they are truly Warriors in the best sense of the word.

I also do not subscribe to some far-right mind-set that would have us all living the hand that is dealt us without the help of society and the government. I believe it is society's responsibility to assist those truly in need, and I am happy to pay taxes that support necessary social services. I support those Warriors who fight for the rights of the disadvantaged by complaining about and tackling injustice. Complaining to effect positive change is not whining, and it is often a technique of the Warrior.

As a culture, we should all be ashamed when we see the truly repressed and mentally ill roaming our streets with nowhere to go, because it is in everyone's best interests to maintain social programs that deal compassionately with those in need. Caring for those who really can't care for themselves is what separates us from beasts, and ultimately, it makes this world a better place for all of us.

THE VICTIM MENTALITY

However, I am concerned about the "cult of irresponsibility" that has been sweeping this nation for the last couple of decades, making it acceptable for people to disguise their own inadequacies, weaknesses, laziness, and blatant social and criminal mistakes under the guise of the "victim's mentality." And although it is human nature to often lose track of how wonderful we have it as we concentrate on those who have it even better, it seems absurd in this wonderful day and age that we can't all at least pause in amazement at the incredible progress mankind has made, and how Americans have especially benefited from this advancement.

As I write this, the United States is at the tail end of the greatest increase in wealth in the history of the world. Although we are most likely entering a period of financial adjustment and equalization that will seem a bit painful in contrast to the easy money times most people experienced during the last decade, there is certainly little reason for most people to whine. We've come so far: we can afford to give a little back.

The American middle- and upper-middle class now lives with luxuries that just a few years ago would have left the world's most elite aristocracy wide-eyed in amazement. Here's a short list of how American society has changed—for the worse, in many respects:

- Millionaires are now a dime a dozen, and the billionaire now occupies the financial status seat.

- After a hard day at the air-conditioned glass palace they call the office, most Americans pop the remote control that allows them electronic access into the leather-trimmed control center of their $35,000 SUV.

- They sip $5 designer coffees as they listen to their five-thousand-watt ten-CD electronic sound system, while cruising at high speeds down immaculately manicured roadways, totally unconcerned about the elements, because their all-wheel drive vehicles have been designed to tackle any road condition.

- They chat with friends on tiny cell phones, pausing to enter lunch and concert dates into handheld computers that help organize their complicated lives.

- They talk about their 401k programs, last night's episode of *Desperate Housewives*, and the newest $700 titanium-enhanced super golf club they are going to buy next week.

Long gone are the days when conversations would be laced with stories of relatives who died from common diseases or in a war. Although medical science can certainly always keep advancing, today's twenty-year-olds can be relatively statistically confident of living to ninety years of age or more, most likely with medicine and genetic therapy that will keep them looking and feeling good, and even sexually active, at ages well past their grandparents' average life span.

And the truth is, I couldn't be happier about all of this. Why not? We deserve it. Although I am not entirely convinced that many so-called advances in society will ultimately prove superior to the ways we did it in the old days, I much prefer a vanilla latte to the caustic Folgers' java I used to buy at the gas station, I really like the way my Range Rover handles, and I look forward to making love to my wife for seven or eight hours on my ninety-fifth birthday. Many talented Warriors and Workers put a lot of effort into innovating and creating this bold new world, and we should enjoy it.

SUCCESS AND PRIVILEGE AREN'T GOD-GIVEN RIGHTS

But in the midst of all this good news, there is a nasty social attitude that concerns me—a mass misunderstanding of what brought us here—looming on the horizon. Instead of enjoying the fruits of our labor, many people take them for granted, and they concentrate on wanting more. They lose track of the fact that we all have to earn the benefits of a great society; they aren't a God-given right that we can abuse. They focus on what they don't have, instead of living in reality. They whine like the annoying spoiled brats that always seem to sit behind me on airplanes, and/or they are raising an entire generation of Whiners who, in a few years, will be running things.

We need future generations of smart and motivated people, who are thankful for the opportunities they have, and who are anxious to leave their marks by making things even better. We don't need legions of spoon-fed Whiners who feel their birthrights include designer clothes and rooms full of consumer electronics, with no responsibility toward others included. And the parents who are creating this generation—although they have the most admirable motivations—need to instill a better sense of community ethics in their kids.

Widespread social acceptance of whining will only lead to a dysfunctional society. It has unfortunately also become acceptable to blame others for our own lack of motivation, talent, mistakes, and/or addictions and criminal abuses that should clearly fall on the person who created the violation or made the mistake. This goes beyond the simple act of an explanation of events that led up to events in questions. I am alarmed and disgusted by society's seeming acceptance of whining as an excuse for actions that should be considered inexcusable under any circumstances and by the trend to placate the Whiner by shifting responsibility to the masses that had no connection to the situation.

TEACH YOUR CHILDREN TO BE RESPONSIBLE

Although they may complain about a disciplined structure, children ultimately crave and admire strong parents who set guidelines and enforce rules. They grow as individuals by achieving goals and fulfilling challenges that are set for them by people they admire. They look to their parents to establish the benchmarks of good citizenship. Parents who avoid the sometimes difficult but necessary dominant position that must be maintained in favor of being an "always-understanding buddy" to their kids do them a great disservice.

If we train children to shirk responsibility, and if we utilize farfetched excuses to explain poor performance, it will haunt them for their entire lives. They'll adopt a Whiner's crutch that will prevent them from realizing their full potential. Parents who exhibit "conflict-avoider" attitudes raise unruly children who ultimately become irresponsible adults.

And parents who shift their own responsibility onto others are teaching their children a terrible lesson. It is increasingly common for parents to transfer many of their parental duties to schools and other outside institutions, perhaps somehow believing that they can simply "hire out" the crucial and often difficult components of parenthood. Although a school is an important part of the process and should be held accountable, school systems and teachers are too often being held responsible for the parents' failings.

Holding children to high standards that parents themselves demonstrate, tempered with understanding and compassion, produces great kids. Holding children responsible for their actions, as opposed to laying the blame on a teacher or other supervising adult, is a great lifelong learning tool for a child. Teaching kids to use the Warrior's tools from an early age gives them a great advantage. Children will be constantly tempted with situations that encourage lack of responsibility and whining as they move through life, and to have the tools in hand to reject the easy way, and persevere with conviction, aggression, and high ethical standards will make them winners—not Whiners—in the long run.

Ultimately, as a society, we particularly admire those who came from adversity to persevere and prosper. We motivate and train our children with stories of our forefathers escaping religious and governmental persecution to form the United States of America, of Abe Lincoln walking miles through the snow just to attend school, of Beethoven creating heavenly sounds despite his deafness, and the many stories of social, political, and business leaders who came from poor and/or disadvantaged backgrounds to achieve greatness.

IT'S OKAY TO WHINE *OCCASIONALLY*

We all have Whiners in our life, and most of us occasionally find a little comfort in doing a little whining. There is nothing wrong with an occasional bout of whining, as there is something a bit cathartic and healthy about expressing our frustrations with a little out-and-out complaining. I sometimes become an insufferable and annoying Whiner (as my wife and employees will undoubtedly verify) when I feel that I am out of control, or when my work schedule has been particularly harrowing. As I manager, I also recognize that sometimes I need to allow employees the opportunity to vent so they can move on in a more productive manner, as long as that does not become a consistent part of our relationship.

But transforming into a true Whiner is an altogether different experience. Many people prefer to purge themselves of any responsibility, and instead lay their unhappiness, lack of success, problems in relationships, and other difficulties on everyone around them. They draw negative attention to themselves, somehow believing that attention for the wrong reasons is better than no attention at all. Living the "Whiner lifestyle" ensures an almost continual state of unhappiness. It is a sure way to avoid success—and the good feelings one gets from accomplishing something on his or her own. After all, if all the problems you may experience are caused by everyone around you, then it is equally difficult to accept the credit for the good that befalls you.

WHINERS CAN EASILY TURN INTO WEASELS

Whiners are also at the dangerous gateway to becoming Weasels, and in fact, at some point, almost every Weasel makes the descent into the black hole after serving a stint as a Whiner. When a person makes the jump to being a Whiner, he or she essentially takes themselves out of the loop of life. Whiners are victims, controlled by the perceived injustice that seems to constantly surround them. Unfortunately, it is a short step from taking no responsibility and placing the blame on others to living a life of deceit and malice.

IT'S NOT TOO LATE TO AVOID BECOMING A WHINER

The good news is that if you are a Whiner or exhibiting Whiner tendencies, it is not too late to change. Self-responsibility ultimately feels good. It puts you in control—clarifies your life—and makes success all the sweeter, because once you realize that you personally control your own destiny, life opens up to you. You experience less stress in life, because you are no longer the victim. You realize that any problem that befalls you is short term in nature, because you can change the situation. Sometimes, it is almost as if you are entering a society that you realize always existed but that you were completely unaware of—a world in which people strive to be happy and enjoy life's pleasures as they progress, instead of the Whiner's world, which is filled with constant dark clouds always threatening to open up and dump on you.

The bottom line is that certainly, we all start life with a wide range of advantages and disadvantages—but what you do with your life ultimately falls into your hands. Good or bad, you own it, so you might as well make the most of it. It's all within your control, and complaining past a certain point will always fall on deaf ears. Whiners need to rechannel the energy they put into lamenting their lot in life into improving their situation. Taking responsibility for your problems puts you in control so you can improve your situation, and it also allows you take credit for life's successes. That's all part of the deal.

• • • • • • • • • • •

In the next chapter, we will cover a "Recipe for Failure" that frequently transforms someone into a Whiner or Weasel.

CHAPTER 12

A Recipe for Failure:
Addictions—and How to Deal
With Them

"Don't blame the booze."
—Auggie Smith, (Stand-Up Comedian)

No single personality trait potentially ensures failure in life and business quite as much as an unchecked addiction. As we saw in chapter 10, Whiners and addiction frequently go hand in hand, because addiction and whining typically always involve some level of self-delusion. We all know addicts, and most of us suffer from some potential or minor addiction that we manage to keep from becoming the focal point of our lives.

But the world is bursting with *true* addicts: people so out of control that they can't stop eating (or not eating and/or vomiting); drinking; and partaking in the ever-widening variety of available drugs, gambling, and dangerous sex, regardless of the consequences. Addictions are nondenominational and insidious, striking Warriors and Workers as well as Whiners and Weasels.

In the interest of full disclosure, I have tried all of the above on many occasions (with the exception of not eating and forced vomiting), so I can certainly understand the appeal, to a point, of all of them. In fact, I especially enjoy . . . well, perhaps I won't go there. But compulsions that cause you to ignore everything else in your life, drive you to abandon relationships, and force you into bad health and poverty should not become a permanent part of your existence. The key to enjoying any vice is *moderation*—and knowing when your system is not built to even experiment with that vice. Addictions are the ultimate self-destructive behavior that spills over to impact everyone around the addict.

ADDICTION IS WIDESPREAD—BUT IT CAN STILL BE OVERCOME

I see the pain and problems of addiction on an almost daily basis. My own family is riddled with addictions that haunt the lives of otherwise wonderful and talented people. I know intelligent counselors who make their living treating addicts, only to then go home to battle their own addictions despite all they know about the subject. Addiction is a major problem in almost every business, as managers take on the role of counselors, helping people see the severity of their own actions, and the ultimate price that will be paid if they don't get themselves under control. I have unfortunately had to fire addicts at every level in their careers, usually after they have completely given up the battle for control and their addictions have sometimes turned them into liars and, in one case, a thief. It is costly, unproductive, emotionally draining, sad for everyone involved, and ultimately, incredibly manipulative of the addict.

And addicts are not the only ones who pay the price for their problem: the burden is also shared by their families, their employers, and their fellow employees. This is the unseen and most selfish side of addiction that most addicts refuse to face: the pain they cause everyone around them. And as the addict begins his or her spiral downwards, society pays the price as we maintain programs to at least keep addicts alive.

THE BENEFIT OF PROFESSIONAL HELP TO OVERCOME ADDICTIONS

I am certainly not qualified to comment on the proper care and treatment of those with addictions. I am pleased to have seen some wonderful recoveries from people who I feared would be lost to their own compulsions.

With outside help, and/or their own personal strength, they rebounded to live terrific lives, so I believe that recovery is possible for everyone, no matter how far they have sunk. There are certainly many productive Warriors and Workers who have conquered their addictions to come roaring back.

But I do want to address the reality of the situation. The current compassionate mind-set is to classify most addictions as *diseases*—a broad classification that I and many true experts in the field do not necessarily agree with. It violates the tenet of *rights = responsibility,* and it minimizes the plight of those suffering from truly uncontrollable conditions. At some point, an addict makes the choice to pursue his or her addiction, which in my mind disqualifies it as a disease. The twenty-five-year-old mother of two who is indiscriminately struck down with cancer and is fighting desperately for her life suffers from a disease. In contrast, I would not classify the fifty-year-old investment banker who has made a conscious decision to abandon his business, family, and health so he can have a close and personal relationship with Jack Daniels in the same category.

Those unexpectedly forced to fight for their lives often become the ultimate Warriors, battling incredible pain, fear, and despair in the hope of living. This stands in stark contrast to many addicts who have the potential for terrific lives but instead choose to give up and let themselves be overtaken by their weaknesses.

Although I would agree that some of us could be genetically or socially predisposed toward altering our chemical composition, donating all of our money to a poker machine or a drug dealer or spending extreme sums and efforts to keep our genitals occupied with strangers does not negate our responsibility to ourselves and society. Given my background as an Irish American with a long lineage of noisy (albeit charming, handsome, and entertaining) gambling alcoholics in the family, I suppose certain members of my gene pool would be more comfortable if I spent my days sitting in a bar betting on football games, while sipping quarts of Guinness and singing catchy Irish ditties.

As I pointed out, addicts also tend to have a high propensity to become Whiners. It is rooted in the unreasonable assumption that addicts have no choice in becoming addicts, which accordingly gives them plenty of reason to complain. I have addicted friends who seem to think that addiction is the norm, and all of us that have not succumbed to our desires are actually the strange ones.

"I learned in my treatment that I was destined to become an alcoholic," one friend in AA told me, "given the fact that both my father and grandfather were drinkers."

"Then why aren't you a plumber?" I inquired of her, "since that is something else they both shared."

ADDICTS NEED TO ACCEPT RESPONSIBILITY FOR THEIR OWN LIVES

If you are an addict, or you find yourself giving in to your compulsions frequently enough that you are considering the idea, you have an important decision to make. Ultimately, the decision will be yours, and I know it won't be an easy one. But you should be pleased that, unlike most other diseases that could befall you, you get a *choice* with this one.

Many of the addicts I know suffer from the pain of guilt associated with their problems. In fact, the guilt often becomes the barrier to their recovery. I can tell you, as someone who has urged a lot of addicts to recover: forget about the guilt. At this point, we are not really focused on what happened in the past when you gambled away your paycheck, spent your daughter's birthday in a vodka-induced fog, vomited in your date's new car, or offended everyone at the company Christmas party by announcing your physical superiority to the boss while dropping your pants to prove the point. (Actually, that particular episode did enhance an otherwise dull evening—but in the end it proved to be a bad idea.)

The question now is whether or not you have the courage and integrity to overcome your addiction—for good. If you do, there will be plenty of time to apologize for past transgressions, and because you were strong enough to win the battle, we will happily accept your apologies as long as you are resolute in your recovery. Seeing you a slave to your addictions is much more difficult than forgiving you if you make the tough choice to recover. There is never a point too late to turn over a new leaf and receive acceptance. Remember, one of the Warrior's tools is *compassion*, and you will find it in abundance when you really beat your demons.

However, to use that guilt as a reason not to get well is just another cop out that further damages your credibility. Beating addiction shares similarities to becoming a Warrior. You have to do it yourself, for your own reasons. It requires self-control, courage, and confidence, and if you are successful, the benefits spread to all those around you. And if you choose not to do it, regardless of what led to your addictions, *you* own your failure. Don't expect limitless patience and understanding from those around you.

. . . .

In the next chapter, we will take a closer look at the world of the Whiner. Get ready to do a little self-analysis to see if you fit the profile in any way.

CHAPTER 13

Are You a Whiner?
Signs to Watch For

"I was not lying. I said things that later seemed to be untrue."
— Richard Nixon

Whining is a bit insidious. It has a tendency to creep up on you, because we all have to do it occasionally. As covered in Chapter 11, a bit of occasional whining can be therapeutic to the soul. It's healthy to occasionally air your complaints and rid yourself of a little anger. But left unchecked or overly encouraged, whining can quickly grow into an energy-draining "attitude cancer" that will hamper your career, drive away or lose friends and loved ones, and relegate you to a constant state of depression. It alters perception: white becomes black, good becomes bad, and the enjoyment is sapped from life. A Whiner's cup always tastes bitter and is at least half empty.

There are a myriad of problems associated with whining, aside from the obvious downside to Whiners and those around them that results from a life spent complaining. Whiners are often constantly depressed because they have no sense of empowerment.

A few days ago my wife pulled me aside to announce that I had been a real Whiner the last few weeks, and it was making her life—and mine—

particularly unpleasant. Of course, this is not news anyone likes to hear, but as I gave it some thought I realized she was right. And in analyzing the problem, I determined that several current factors were making me feel particularly out of control. We were in the midst of building a new house that had spiraled a little out of control, a real estate project I had in development was well past deadline and exceeding budget, deadlines for this book were looming, and I generally felt that I was not on top of my game. Accordingly, I had become a whiny pain-in-the-ass and was making my employees and family miserable! People are at their best and most confident when they feel in control of their destiny, and controlling your destiny is certainly one of the mantras of this book.

RECOGNIZE THE PSYCHOLOGICAL SOURCE OF WHINING—AND ITS MANIFESTATIONS AND EFFECTS

Whining is an admission of a lack of control. Whiners complain they can't advance in their job because "the man" won't let them. Whiners never actually admit their advancement is primarily dependent on their own performance. A Whiner complains about government—but in the same breath admits that he or she don't vote because "it doesn't make a difference," and, of course, they never get personally involved to improve the situation. Whining says to the world that you do not have the talent, power, and/or will to make your life the best it can be. It is the easy way out. Instead of taking the self-responsibility to improve their lot in life and solve the problems and issues that hold them back, Whiners shift the responsibility to everyone else. Whining is a proclamation that you have been beaten by your life and the system. Your job, family, friends, and almost everyone and everything else you come into contact with have the power to control you. You are simply a slave to all that surrounds you, and the only power you possess is the power to complain.

And to compound the situation is the depression that accompanies it. Whiners often have a limited social life, which can become very lonely. Certainly, nobody enjoys being around Whiners, because they tend to be so focused on their own situation that a conversation with them is completely one-sided ("so enough about me, now let's talk about what is really bothering me and why I'm not happy"). Most Whiners have gone through a progression of complaining throughout their lives that ultimately brought them to their Whiner status. Their friends either tend to be from the "old days," before they became so insufferable, or other Whiners who can't find any other decent companionship.

Whiners are under the mistaken belief that their complaints will bring them positive pity and attention from others. In reality, it just serves to isolate them, and at some point, the pity from others transforms to disgust when they realize the Whiner suffers from constant self-pity as opposed to some real malady or unfortunate situation.

Whining has the "crying wolf" effect. Those around a Whiner become immune to his or her complaints, so if the Whiner truly is encountering a bad situation, his or her friends and coworkers tend to minimize the situation. Whiners tap out the normally available emotional support systems that surround them, so they aren't available when they really need them.

And if they aren't talking about themselves, Whiners tend to be complaining about other people's successes, focusing on how *unfair* it is that they don't enjoy the same satisfactions in life. Typically, Whiners focus on an excuse: the "I-coulda'-been-a-contender" syndrome. They will explain ad nauseam about how they are qualified for something, but they just "didn't get the breaks like a lot of other people," so they are relegated to doing something they don't like. Just being around a Whiner is depressing and draining.

WHINERS CAN POISON OTHERS—AND DO SERIOUS DAMAGE TO THEMSELVES

Accordingly, past a certain point, only other Whiners and dysfunctional people stay in the Whiner's circle, which just adds to the problem. When Whiners surround themselves with other Whiners, it gives the entire group the false impression that their actions and attitudes are normal, and they begin to feed off each other. Whiners typically also suffer from mild to advanced degrees of paranoia. It is an easy jump to go from "oh, poor me" to "the world is out to get me." It all leads to an endless circle of misery for the Whiner—or at least that's what they believe.

Whiners are also prime candidates to take the next self-destructive step into various addictions (as discussed in chapters 11 and 12). Although all Whiners certainly do not become obese, alcoholics, drug addicts, gamblers, or sexually addicted, most addicted people are Whiners. They justify their addictions with the usual Whiner excuses about all that drove them to bet, gorge themselves, drink, snort, smoke, swallow, or frequently get naked with absolute strangers. They rationalize that they somehow "feel things" more strongly than others, which gives them license to give in to various weaknesses, usually leaving others to pay the toll for them. They feel they suffer from a social disease, and accordingly, they expect society to fund the damage they leave in their wake—as well as their treatment.

THE REST OF US PAY FOR
THE WHINER'S WAY OF LIFE

Society really has no recourse. The rest of us have to pay for Whiners' excesses, to protect our own way of life. Of course, there are many people who will take great offense at this statement, perhaps correctly citing the fact that many addicted people do suffer from legitimate diseases that have made them much more susceptible to various addictions. But giving this position too much acceptance creates an acknowledgment of social acceptance that we cannot allow. Individuals need to be held accountable, despite their troubled histories. We are much better advised to publicly celebrate the success of those who faced difficulties and persevered, as opposed to just accepting lack of self-control and allowing it to become a social norm.

Of course, not all Whiners reach those extremes. They range from the mildly annoying and negative to the truly societally destructive, and everywhere in between. One of the most unfortunate aspects of most Whiners' situations is that they already possess the skill sets to achieve their goals; they just misuse their tools and allow themselves to fall into such a state of self-pity and self-destructiveness that they never improve their situations.

WHINERS WHO BELIEVE IN THE LOTTERY
LIFESTYLE

I also find that many Whiners at some point put their trust into fate, as opposed to anything that they perceive they control. Fate allows Whiners to free themselves of responsibility. It is much easier to say, "I'm not successful because my parents made me that way, or because I wasn't born in the right time and place" as opposed to "I'm not successful because I didn't work hard enough" or "I'm not successful because I did not exercise a little self-control when needed." Whiners perceive that they are almost always the *victims* of something they personally could not control, and they believe that successful people are the recipient of some random benefit, as opposed to action they took to make themselves successful.

This attitude also translates into making them big believers in "the lottery lifestyle." It is comforting and nonthreatening for Whiners to believe they had no real choice in the big scope of things, as opposed to the pressure of knowing we all ultimately control our destinies. The biggest problem with living the lottery lifestyle is that it releases believers from the necessary sense of discipline and planning that would help them achieve their goals in life.

Denis is a prime example of the long-term negative impact of trusting in fate instead of yourself. On the surface, it appears that Denis, a school counselor, has built a fulfilling life helping people. He is almost always fun and pleasant to be around, and he seems to be the eternal optimist.

But spend a few minutes with him, and you will soon discover that he is a classic example of someone living the lottery lifestyle. In his heart, Denis always dreamed of living the life of the idle rich, traveling around the world. He spends a lot of time reading about "the lucky ones," as he likes to refer to successful people. In fact, he has often said to me, "What does it feel like to be so lucky?"

I explain to Denis that, although a little occasional good fortune does make life's challenges easier to bear, I like to think that my own success is a result of the right attitude, hard work, and perseverance. I also point out that luck had little to do with the success stories he loves to devour, and that those individuals almost always achieved their success by using their Warrior tools.

But this is not the solution Denis is seeking, because if he accepts it, then *the onus is on him* to improve his life. Instead, Denis prefers to gamble in the hope of hitting it rich. Almost every day, Denis religiously invests in several lottery tickets, certain that someday his number will hit. Once or twice a month, he drives one hundred miles to a casino, plunking down his limited and hard-earned dollars into a poker machine. The by-product of all this is that Denis is constantly walking a financial tightrope, barely able to stay afloat, much less put anything away for his retirement, which is looming just a few years away. This leaves him depressed, which leads to a host of other problems.

The saddest part of Denis's situation is that there is a simple and almost painless solution that could radically improve his life. Sometimes, all the solutions you really need are right in front of you—you just need to take them. Instead of spending time concentrating on how he could suddenly become "lucky," Denis should develop and orchestrate a plan to live his life to its fullest and create his own success. The $5 a day he spends on lottery tickets and the $200 to $300 he gambles away every month at the casino could translate into more than $5,000 a year in her savings account.

The main reason Denis wants to be rich is to travel, and with the extra time he would have from not visiting the casinos, he could research and plan yearly vacations that he would now be able to afford. Plus, he could still put away some of the money into a retirement program to give him added peace of mind. And although he would not be traveling in the lap of luxury, he would be fulfilling a life's desire and creating something that he could look forward to and attain. He would eliminate the stress and guilt of his gambling and the financial problems that are a result of the addiction. What if Denis is really ambitious? Time not spent in casinos or dreaming about jackpots could be put to better use in a part-time weekend job doing something he really enjoyed, which would allow him to build a bigger retirement kitty, gain some new interests in his life, and perhaps travel in a more luxurious style.

THE SILENT WHINERS

I also frequently run into another variation on the condition: the Silent Whiner. This type can be a bit more deceptive. Silent Whiners often appear to be silently strong, not really complaining, but simply enduring the somewhat hazy problems and disadvantages that life seems to have dealt them. But they are simply internalizing their lack of control and their belief that life continues to deal them a bad hand that they cannot escape.

They spend a lot of time whining in private, to themselves and their closest friends and family members. Their life is frequently a litany of excuses for why they are not where they want to be, and they seem to take some perverse pleasure in being the stoic victim. Instead of being known for their accomplishments and talents, they prefer to be admired for having a strong face during adversity. And because this is their trademark, they actually seek out adversity so they can play the victims. This might be admirable if they were really dealing with uncontrollable situations, but most typically, they are just seeking excuses for their inability to muster the fortitude to move forward in their lives and master their destiny.

Shirley is a good example of a Silent Whiner. She was raised in a relatively privileged household with supportive siblings, and whatever education she would choose and could qualify for was made available to her.

But Shirley suffered from insecurity from an early age. Somewhat of a follower by nature, she quickly fell in with the quintessential wrong crowd, and her life came to a fifteen-year standstill. She started and quit college many times, squandering the easy opportunities her family made available. Every couple of years, Shirley starts a new career with great flourish and ambition, but within a few months, she has lost her enthusiasm or quit the job.

Rather than address her inability to fit in, she always has an excuse (or rather accusation) about the institution or company she is abandoning. "The professors at the college were not as good as promoted. I really couldn't learn from them. The other students were snobs. I have decided that I want to dedicate my life to public service. I decided I couldn't work in a place full of bureaucrats. I'm creative and need to work in a creative environment. I can't work around those people—just because they think they are creative, they are snobs." Etc, etc.

And as a Silent Whiner, Shirley only expressed her opinions to a few select people. To the outside world, she just seems like a kind but troubled person, truly searching for her lot in life. The problem now is that Shirley is in her mid-thirties, but her attitude has not changed from adolescence. She believes that life owes her something special, but instead of applying herself and working to achieve it, she just keeps wandering and quietly complaining. And the longer she has to search, the unhappier and further from her goal she becomes.

Silent Whiners need to take a different approach from traditional Whiners. In fact, they need to come public with their complaints, cleanse their souls of the real or perceived problems or injustices that they feel have hampered their lives, and then move on to bigger and better things and a happier life. Once exorcised from the problems and excuses, they are forced to deal with reality and confront their problems. If you don't speak up, you can't effect change. But the key is to first make sure the problems you perceive are real and valid, and then address them in the proper manner.

Once they have aired and abandoned their excuses, Silent Whiners need to take the same path that all Whiners should take to elevate themselves from their unhappy existences. They need to regard life with optimism—and the attitude that they are in complete control of their destiny.

WHINERS CAN DESTROY A WORKPLACE—
BUT A SAVVY MANAGER CAN SAVE IT

Whiners are not only annoying, but they can often be quite destructive to the workplace and social environments. One needs to be on particular guard for the "Opinionator"—that whiny individual who, despite his or her sour personality, has managed to become somewhat of a leader. Typically, these are Whiners who gain a following among other Whiners and individuals on the cusp of becoming Whiners. They spew forth a steady stream of negativity and complaints, and even though there is seldom much truth to what they say, their continual whining can often turn an otherwise healthy environment into a cauldron of dissatisfaction. It is essential to immediately identify these kinds of people, and either work with them to change their positions to something more positive, or eliminate them from the group before irreparable damage is done.

For example, a friend of mine faced this situation a few years ago when she took a new position in charge of a department of seventy-five employees. Her new boss had warned my friend that morale and performance were at dangerously low levels in the department, and her charge was to fix the situation.

After spending a week meeting with the employees and reviewing operations, it became clear to my friend that there were three Opinionators who were spearheading the anti-company attitude. While she discovered the employees had some valid points of dissatisfaction, these were problems that could easily be solved. For the most part, the dissatisfaction was the result of the constant complaining and rumor-mongering of a few. After meeting individually with the three, my friend surmised there was one clear leader (a serious Whiner bordering on becoming a Weasel), and that the other two could most likely be swayed into a more pro-company position with proper handling.

My friend's first step was to invite the two to lunch and ask their opinion about how to improve operations. At first, they complained without offering solutions (a classic Whiner response), but as the conversation progressed and my friend offered possible solutions, she began to sway them. Finally, she got the two to agree to head up a committee to implement the changes, which, in effect, isolated them from the head Whiner.

Because they now had responsibility, they couldn't really complain, and they began to take a pro-company stance that soon spread through the department.

Empowering a Whiner to change the problem they whine about is often a great way to change their attitude—assuming you can get them to accept the responsibility. Although the head Whiner was somewhat neutered, she continued her negativity, and within a few weeks, my friend found sufficient cause to fire her. Had she done this when the Whiner held power, it could have been disastrous, but once the employees began to enjoy a more positive environment, they had no desire to fall back into negativity.

My friend continued to streamline and improve her department, and over the next year, she laid off a few additional Weasels and Whiners who were polluting the work environment. In the end, she created a great work environment that employees appreciated, and as a result, she increased productivity and profits.

WHEN WHINING IS THE CORPORATE CULTURE

Sometimes, entire organizations are formed around whining, with a business model partially structured on whining as a profit center. For instance, a friend of mine runs a small interior design firm. I know from experience that his modus operandi is to bid projects low so he is awarded the work, and then he quickly builds a good personal relationship with the owners.

After a few weeks of work, he begins to complain about all the extras he and his staff are including for the "extremely low price" he bid the project. He has the right kind of personality to be endearing while whining. Of course, he fails to mention that all the work was supposed to be included in the price, and instead, he creates the illusion that the client is receiving an enormous amount of extra time that "could never have been logically included in the original bid," just because he is so "captivated by the project." And he has trained his staff to reinforce his whining when they are around the client. "Oh, my poor boss, he has been working day and night on your design, because he just loves you and the project so much!"

Usually, the client caves in, often paying a premium of 25–50 percent over the original bid, just to shut him up and make him happy. And unfortunately, because this tactic works for him, he keeps it up. The problem is that even though he does wonderful work, a large percentage of his clients feel badly about their experience after everything is completed, and his work is tainted with his whining. Instead of being known for the quality of his work, his whining for more money becomes the legacy of the project, which fails to make anyone happy with the work experience.

I emphasize here that Whiners may very well have the talent and capabilities to achieve their goals and happiness; they just unconsciously choose not to. Whining has nothing to do with a lack of anything—except perspective and self-respect. At its essence, whining is a symptom of a lack of confidence, self-respect, and fortitude. And although Whiners may often be insufferable and negative, they are often not bad people, and they should not be confused with Weasels. In fact, many of my good friends are Whiners, to some degree.

The good news is that Whiners can eliminate their bad habits for their own good and the good of those around them. If an employee, friend, or loved one is a Whiner, it is certainly worth the attempt to try and rehabilitate them for their own sake and the sake of all those around them. If you know someone who is making the transition to becoming a Whiner, bring it to his or her attention. Make them read this chapter. My wife and I are on constant "Whiner's Check" for each other. When one of us steps over the line, as happens frequently, the other kiddingly (but with serious intentions) says, "Hmmm, aren't we becoming the Whiner?" which usually whips us back into shape.

WHINING IS A CHOICE— BUT YOU CAN CHANGE IT

Most Whiners maintain reasonable ethical positions in their lives; they just make the choice to be miserable. In fact, I have known many talented and successful Whiners who had everything in life—except the correct attitude to enjoy it. One of my oldest friends is such a person. Bill was raised in a good household, by reasonably well-adjusted parents. He is educated and financially sound, and he enjoys a lucrative and fulfilling career as an attorney. But unfortunately for Bill, he is also a lifelong Whiner: always existing within a mythical black cloud of despair that he believes surrounds him. Despite the fact that he is in wonderful shape, his mental condition even manifests itself physically. He always seems a bit hunched over, his face scrunched up as if he were enduring a weeklong headache. He frequently complains of the aches and pains and headaches that we all feel occasionally, but that most of us usually choose to ignore.

Those who know Bill have learned never to ask him how he is doing, because the answer is always a depressing and drawn-out monologue of all the bad that he believes befalls him. "God, my new client is just a terror," Bill laments—forgetting to mention that the new client will help pay for his new sports car. "I pulled a muscle playing tennis," he complains sourly—not thinking about the fact that he is sore after spending a few hours engrossed in his favorite sport at a swanky club. "My God-awful sister and her boring husband are visiting this weekend," he sighs—totally missing the point that he has a devoted family member who loves him and for some strange reason enjoys spending time with him.

Of course, Bill does have his high points. He occasionally crawls out of his black hole and lets the many aspects of his personality shine that originally attracted all of his friends to him. He treats us to rare glimpses of his intelligence and wit for an hour or an evening, only to ultimately withdraw again into the Whiner's existence for no apparent reason.

I have discussed all this with him, but instead of attempting to emerge from his perceived misery, he just has a myriad of lame excuses that often cross over into the ridiculous. "My parents were cold and unloving when I grew up. I didn't get into my first choice of colleges. I don't make as much money as my brother. My wife is too career-oriented. My wife is not career-oriented enough. The partners don't like me. Blah, blah, blah."

It's important that all of us occasionally take a "Whiner check" to make sure that we aren't becoming a Bill. Certainly we all go through "whiny" phases in life, but it is essential to stay in check to make sure we aren't making the leap to living life as a Whiner. Take a look at the following "Whiner's Checklist" to see how many statements you agree with, and c'mon, be honest. This is just between us. (For the full interactive Whiner's test, go to www.warriorsandweasels.com.)

THE WHINER'S CHECKLIST

Here are some typical Whiners' complaints and rationales for why their lives are the way they are. Do any apply to you (or anyone you know)?

- ❏ "I think I would be happier and more successful in life if my parents had given me better guidance (or financial or emotional support, or more hugs, or my own room, or a car on my sixteenth birthday)."

- ❏ "I can't help being the way I am because that is the way I was raised."

- ❏ "My lack of education (or the bad teachers I had, or the school I attended) has really held me back in my career."

- ❏ "I really have to blame my dad (or Mom, or both, or spouse, or boyfriend/girlfriend, or kids, or siblings) for the lack of progress in my life and/or career."

- ❏ "My boss (or teachers, or coworkers) doesn't see my full potential."

- ❏ "My boss got his/her job by kissing up to the big boss, not because he/she is particularly talented."

- ❏ "I am constantly discriminated against because I'm [pick one: black, white, blonde, not blonde, Hispanic, Arab, Indian, Asian, a woman, a man, gay, not gay, Jewish, not Jewish, not attractive, too attractive, too young, too nerdy, too old, too fat, too skinny, too short, too tall, not hip enough, too hip, too busty, not busty enough, didn't go to the right school, don't have an MBA, have an MBA, too sexy, not sexy enough, smarter than they are and they resent it, the driver of a great car, from the wrong side of the tracks, misunderstood, too direct, not direct enough]."

- ❏ "I realize that if truth were told, people actually fear me, and that's the reason I have not achieved all that I want."

❏ "Even though I don't like what I'm doing, I'm too old to do anything else. I have to worry about my security."

❏ "My [pick one: brother, sister, friend, coworker, college roommate, best friend] has it made because they are [richer, better looking, have richer parents, date the boss, sleep around, are more aggressive, are luckier] than I am."

❏ "Most of the people I work around are idiots. I'm the smartest one here, and if I ran this company, we would really get things done."

❏ "If people understood me better, they would realize what I am really capable of."

❏ "Most successful people got that way because they had rich parents [relatives, friends] who helped them."

❏ "Life is a bit like the lottery—some people are just lucky enough to win."

❏ "Right now I am just "putting in time" at my job until I move on to something I will really enjoy and be good at." (This is an especially bad one if you are over forty.)

❏ "When I tell people about my work history, I also have to explain to them the factors that have prevented me from becoming more successful (e.g., my last boss didn't like me, my coworkers felt threatened by me, the company was screwed up, they put me in the wrong position, they were on the verge of bankruptcy and I came along too late to save them, etc.)."

❏ "I [pick one: smoke, gamble too much, drink too much, take drugs, date/marry abusive people, eat too much and am fat, eat and vomit so I am skinny and unhealthy, fool around on my spouse] because I like to live that way, and it is nobody's business."

❏ "One of these days, someone will realize how talented I am, and then everything will change for me."

❏ "Nothing is ever going to change for me, because life is really just unfair, and some people get all the breaks. I'm just not one of them."

❑ "I'm not in control."

WHAT TO DO IF YOU'RE A WHINER

So how many of the above statements do you agree with? Well, if you said "yes" to even one, you might be on the road to becoming a Whiner. Two or more, and you are already there. But don't lose hope. Redemption is right around the corner (or at least in the next few chapters).

CHAPTER 14

A Recipe for Failure: How "The Loudmouth" Can Derail Your Career (and Your Personal Relationships)

"If you can't say something nice, don't say anything."
—My Dad, and probably yours

Almost everyone likes to gossip. There is something particularly delicious about a terrific rumor that only you know: the exquisite pain of trying to keep it in, the relief and satisfaction when you quietly spew it out, and finally, the pure delight as your words bring looks of shock and amazement to your enraptured audience.

Of course, the downside to gossiping is the potential pain it can cause you and others. There is nothing more embarrassing than being caught either violating someone's trust, or even worse, spreading blatant lies. Yuck, all of a sudden you are looking suspiciously Weasel-like!

In fact, now that I think about it, gossiping shares a lot of similarities to a bad attack of gas. How you handle it, control it, and choose to spread it around ultimately says a lot about your personal qualities and consideration of others.

BEWARE THE NEGATIVE EFFECTS OF GOSSIPING

We often don't stop to think about the full implications of gossiping. After all, it's fun, and it's one of those human frailties that most of us succumb to now and then. Personally, my occasional inability to control my big mouth is a consistent source of pain and embarrassment that I am constantly striving to gain better control over. I suspect it will be a lifelong battle.

But we all know people who have completely given up the fight. They run off their mouths with wild abandon, either in the common annoying way that identifies them as Whiners, the more insidious way that brands them as untrustworthy, or with the out-of-control approach that makes them chatter as if possessed. And although we all know these kind of people, we probably don't stop to think about the problems their lack of discretion is causing them. Unfortunately, I know a lot of lovely, talented people who possess many or all of the necessary attributes of success in the workplace and in social positions, except for the fact that they continue to be identified as loudmouths.

BEING DISCREET AND LISTENING TO OTHERS HELPS YOUR CAREER

As any manager will tell you, *discretion* among employees is among the most desired attributes. I have had many employees who were terrific at their jobs, but for some reason, they felt inclined to spend large portions of their day gossiping about the company, competitors, and their coworkers, or otherwise pontificating to everyone who will listen about their viewpoints. Their facts are usually wrong, and they are almost always disruptive to the work flow. Sometimes, their actions are serious enough that they have to be officially disciplined, and I have even seen legal action taken as a result of cruel gossip. Unfortunately, even if it is not bad enough to be called out, a lack of discretion can create the unsaid black mark that can haunt someone's career.

There is also a less offensive but equally damaging breed of loudmouth out there—the individual who might not spread rumors but is still incapable of listening and/or talking with a modicum of discretion. I have had many employees who suffered from this affliction. They were all terrific, smart, talented people who, perhaps due to nervousness or insecurity, tend to talk nonstop when put in front of a crowd. It is almost as if they have completely lost their ability to listen. They babble nonstop, often only pausing to emit a loud nervous laugh. The listeners are sometimes amused or occasionally even charmed, but more often, they tend to quickly adopt a puzzled and glazed-over look. It makes it impossible for me to put them in front of many clients, which accordingly places a limitation on their growth in the organization.

This is a deadly mistake to make in the business world. The most effective communicators I know are great listeners who use their ability to quickly sum up situations and then make concise recommendations. They bond with their clients and suppliers by engaging in valuable two-way discussions that result in true relationships. They may be great storytellers and have the ability to transform mundane talk into entertaining conversations, but they also understand that leading the conversation is not always the best approach. They listen and accurately read the crowd to determine if it is more appropriate to be the leader or the attentive listener. And when they do speak, it is with substance. Remember: *Talk less— say more.*

LEARNING TO LISTEN ENHANCES PERSONAL RELATIONSHIPS, TOO

Allowing for two-way conversations as opposed to your own ongoing monologue is also great advice in personal situations. Years ago in my dating days, an attractive woman I was attempting to woo made a comment that was valid at the time to me. "You don't have to fill every gap in the conversation with conversation," she said, observing my nervous chatter. "Sometimes silence can be sexy."

And frequently on other dates, I often found myself praying for a little silence when I would meet women who felt compelled to talk nonstop from the minute I picked them up to the time I dropped them off —often to fill me in on the intimate details of former relationships, but taking absolutely no time to find out anything about me.

A good rule of thumb, whether communicating personally or for business, is to ask yourself after the meeting: "What do I know about them and what do they know about me?" If the communication was one way, one of you will be a mystery. And it they are a mystery to you, you probably made a mistake.

LOUDMOUTHS ARE OFTEN CLUELESS ABOUT THEIR PROBLEM

And here is the tough part. Most of the offenders I know would be completely surprised to learn that their personal brand includes "loudmouth." If you find yourself gossiping or spreading confidential information on a regular basis, you should count on the fact that you are most likely considered untrustworthy, and it has or will hamper your career and your friendships. Most managers will absolutely refuse to elevate someone into a position of power that they cannot take into their confidence. But because this is a sensitive situation to broach and a personality trait widely considered impossible to change, they most likely will never tell you that the reason you did not get the promotion is because you are a loudmouth. Instead, you will increasingly not be included in important discussions because you cannot be trusted.

If you lack the ability to listen, and if you find yourself completely dominating every discussion, I can guarantee you that people have already noticed, and whether you know it or not, it is affecting your life in negative ways.

HOW TO CHANGE YOUR WAYS

The upside to this situation is the opportunity it presents. Regardless of your other skills in the workplace and in friendships, discretion and the ability to be a good listener are qualities we all have the immediate ability to master. If you are working in a marketing or sales position, this is a particularly great talent.

As anyone that knows me would tell you—I can be a talker. Left to my own devices, I feel quite comfortable dominating a conversation with long, overly detailed stories that seem fascinating to me, but could potentially leave the crowd in a sleepy stupor. But one approach that has been helpful to me has been to attempt to channel my chatty ways into real conversations. When dealing with clients, I am particularly careful to lead with questions that should naturally transform to conversations, which keeps me in check. In an ideal situation, I discover that we share interests, which ultimately is satisfying for all of us and the potential basis for an easy and enjoyable long-term relationship. But the key is to balance the questions with discussion—so the process does not feel like an interrogation to the client. If all has gone well, when I take a "knowledge inventory" after our time together, I will almost always know the following, depending of course on how long we were together (and ideally, the client will have this same information about me):

- Where the client is from, where he or she was raised, and his or her family situation.

- Some of his or her employment history.

- How he or she came to be in the business he or she is in.

- People in common we both know.

- Nonwork passions—reading, film, cooking, traveling, family, etc.

We also will both have a good feel for each other's personal brands, our respective senses of humor, and how our future interaction will progress.

If the client knows all of the above about you, and you know little or nothing about the client, then you either have dealt with an incredibly shy person (and that is rare as almost everyone likes to talk about themselves)— or you have been a loudmouth all evening. Taking the inventory helps keep things in check.

. . . .

In the next chapter, we will examine a few other techniques to avoid adopting the even more serious attributes of the Whiner.

CHAPTER 15

Get Over It!
Five Rules to Live By to Avoid Being a Whiner

"I find that the harder I work, the more luck I seem to have."
— Thomas Jefferson

Okay, are you ready for some hard realities in life? If you answered affirmatively to two or more questions on the Whiner's Checklist in chapter 13, then it is probably time to face a little reality. You are a Whiner or well on you're way to becoming something you really don't want to be. And if you passed the Whiner's test with flying colors, you probably already know that the following rules are true.

RULE #1: NOBODY OWES YOU ANYTHING

In a perfect world, we would all have had supportive and loving parents, family members, friends, and coworkers. But right now, although things are the best they have ever been, they aren't perfect. Realizing this is the first step to escape the Whiner's crutch. If you are one of the many who are single-handedly fighting your way out of poverty and/or a disadvantaged background, success will be all the sweeter. Hopefully, you were fortunate to encounter at least a few people and programs that were help-ful, but the truth is that you ultimately control your destiny.

People find success and happiness from every background and walk of life. Although many individuals have enjoyed the benefits of a great up-bringing and education, unfortunately, nobody is automatically entitled to it in today's society. And showing resentment and anger against all of society for the injustices you suffered (or perceived you suffered) will do nothing to make you happy and achieve your goals. Making yourself or others miserable won't solve the problem. Instead, develop a strategy and plan that will ultimately make you content.

Of course, we should all strive to be the parent, friend, spouse, boss, and/or coworker to others that we wish for, and we can all work for the day that every child does receive the guaranteed benefits we would all have hoped to enjoy, but let's deal with the here and now. If you live your life filled with anger and/or regret because you feel you were slighted by other people, or you somehow missed your birthright, then you are a Whiner and you need to get over it!

I can guarantee you that a high percentage of the successful people you admire (or perhaps envy) had it a lot worse than you did. And those who on the surface seem to have enjoyed a lifetime of unearned privilege un-doubtedly have their own issues to address. Besides, success is all the sweeter when you are personally responsible for every aspect of it.

If you want it—earn it yourself. The reality is that your tragic back-ground or the unsupportive cast of characters from your past only buys you a modicum of consideration. There are a lot of sad stories out there, and ultimately, *you* totally control whether or not you make it.

Communication Is Critical. It is not the responsibility of your boss, teacher, or friends to make sure you are appreciated or understood; in-stead, you need to *communicate* with them. For instance, when I hire new employees, one of the facts I make clear to them is that they need to com-municate their career desires to me. The employee and I both need to understand our responsibilities in order to maximize our potential together. My job is to run the company profitably and smoothly so everyone can make a living, and to provide a good work environment so everyone is productive. It is also my responsibility to spot talented people and mentor and elevate them to make the organization more efficient and profitable and achieve the above goals.

But while counseling people to develop them is a part of my job, my primary responsibility is not to be a career counselor, a mind reader, nor am I in the sole business of making everyone around me happy and wealthy. It is the boss's responsibility to *create the structure* that hopefully allows the opportunity for this to occur, and foster talent within the structure with the proper training and reward system. But businesses are not schools dedicated to simply training employees. It is employees' responsibility to *properly communicate their career desires and hidden talents* that might not be immediately apparent to their supervisors.

Over the years, I have had many employees complain to everyone but me that they were not advancing in their careers the way they wanted to, which did them no good and ultimately was a strike against them. If you want a raise, a promotion, a career opportunity, or some kind of acknowledgment you feel you are entitled to or suited for in the workplace, then state your case to your supervisor in a clear, compelling, and factual manner. Avoid emotion and stick to the facts. It is your responsibility to sell yourself and to support your case with facts and figures. Don't whine to others and take no action.

When I conduct a performance review for an employee, I expect it to be a two-way street, with my street taking precedence. I first review the employee's performance, give him or her suggestions on areas of improvement, and help set goals the employee needs to achieve to continue his or her advancement in the company. I then ask the employee for suggestions on how he or she can do his or her job better, improvements I could make in the operation toward achieving this goal, and overall how the company might improve its performance.

Ideally, the employees should respond to this input, offer their own good input, and then sell themselves to me if they are seeking some opportunity. If they feel they deserve more (a raise, a better position, an opportunity to advance), they need to make their case with logical facts, not emotion. If you are going to state a problem, be prepared to present a possible solution; otherwise, you are just whining. If an employee has suggestions on how to improve the company, I want to hear them. It doesn't do any good to grumble to other employees about how things should change. When you quit whining and search for solutions, you realize you possess all the power to achieve your goals. That's a wonderful feeling, certainly preferable to the victim's mentality that usually accompanies being a Whiner.

RULE #2: YOU POSSESS THE CONTROL OVER YOUR LIFE AND SUCCESS

Accept the fact you are not going to win the lottery, or hit a slot machine for a million dollars. Chances are that George Lucas is not going to run into you in a Starbucks and suddenly cast you as the new Hans Solo in his latest film. You are better advised to forget about the "lottery lifestyle" and instead concentrate on how to personally control your destiny. Your dreams of the perfect life, with all the toys and the wonderful relationships and family, will only become a reality *if you make it so*. Any random good luck that befalls you will just be a welcome and unexpected icing on the cake. And the good news about understanding this is that it places all that you desire within your reach, instead of betting your future with astronomical odds against you.

Complaining about your job to your family or coworkers won't change it. Jumping around from school to school—or job to job—won't solve your problems. Decide what you want, and work toward achieving it. Complete a task before jumping to the next one, even if you have lost your interest. Even if completing it does not at first blush seem important to your ultimate goal, it is best to finish it with pride. You don't want to build a history comprised of "giving up," but rather a catalog of achievements that may be helpful to you in the future. I often turn to lessons I learned earlier in my career that were discovered doing things that have absolutely nothing to do with my current profession. Life and professional skills bridge many professions.

Don't depend on anyone else to help you get there. If, along the road, a mentor or some other helpful individual crosses your path, then consider yourself more fortunate than most, and try to pass the benefit on to someone else when you are able. But don't base your entire life's plan on factors that others control.

If you want to make a million dollars or be at the top of your profession, then work hard, make the appropriate sacrifices, take the requisite risks, and develop and follow a long-term plan to achieve your goals. If you want to be famous, approach it like you would any career. Develop your skills, work hard, make the connections, and follow a plan. As I have emphasized before, *use your Warrior's tools*, even if you aren't a Warrior.

And don't allow yourself to be limited by the limitations of others. Whiners tend to attract and often recruit other Whiners. Don't fall into this trap. You will always be known by the company you keep, and if you surround yourself with Whiners, you will soon adopt their habits—and their bad reputations.

RULE #3: ALWAYS CONCENTRATE ON "YOU," NOT "THEM"

Obsessing about others won't get you where you want to go. Certainly, it is valuable to occasionally analyze others' success and failures to give you guidance on how to avoid mistakes, and how you might move forward more effectively. But many people get so immersed in how *everyone else* did it that they forget to move forward with *their own* talents and ideas. There is a big difference between learning from others' successes and obsessing over them. Obsessing about how others did it—and especially whether or not they deserved their success—is an easy road to becoming a Whiner.

"Weasel obsession" or living your life limited by fear is another potential pitfall to avoid. Face the fact that you will encounter many Weasels over your lifetime. They will lie, steal, and take advantage of you in every way possible. Weasels will always be there, lurking in the shadows. It is *your* obligation to minimize their impact. If you live your life in fear or waste time taking extraordinary measures to protect yourself, you will let that distract you from your true goals.

Think of a Weasel as you would a cold or the flu. You have had them before, and you will have them again, and it is certainly not worth worrying about the fact that sometime in the future, you will be sick for a day or two. Stay as healthy as possible, practice good hygiene, and don't worry about it.

Weasels will come from all walks of life, ranging from the pickpocket you will hopefully not meet, to the so-called friend or family member you will definitely encounter who spends years trying to take advantage of you. If you become obsessed thinking about the Weasels that damaged you, or the Weasels in your future, you allow them to win. Focusing on revenge against a Weasel can easily transform you into something you don't want to be.

Learn from bad experiences so you are better protected in the future, and chalk up all the negative encounters you have had with Weasels to valuable learning experiences. Follow the suggestions later in the book on how to Weasel-proof yourself. Don't live life with fear, regrets, or anger. Celebrate others' successes with grace and goodwill, and it will be returned to you when you are successful.

RULE #4: AVOID "ANALYSIS PARALYSIS"

Many people fall into the trap of analysis paralysis, over-thinking situations instead of taking action. Analysis paralysis leads to excuses for not completing a task, which ultimately becomes a form of whining. Although it is important to make decisions based on sound forethought and research and with a complete understanding of all the factors involved, it is essential to, at some point, finally make a decision and stick to it for a reasonable amount of time. Take the jump, or don't complain about the fact that you never reached the heights you desired. I find this an incredibly common problem among individuals, and even businesses. Lack of movement often becomes synonymous with failure.

Analysis Paralysis Is Learned Behavior. It usually starts early in life. We probably all had friends in college who changed majors five or six times in an effort to "find themselves." Usually, this translated into an extra two or three expensive years spent in college, with no perceivable benefit (unless one considers mastering slacking and various drinking games a benefit). This fear of making a decision often continues into adulthood, resulting in either constant delays in life or continual changes that hamper progress. Some people are so afraid of making the *wrong decision* that they make *no decision*, or they make decisions too quickly because they overanalyze a situation.

My good friend Charles is a perfect example. Undecided about his future, he spent six years in college, constantly switching majors, and finally graduating with an undergraduate degree in film. Much to his dismay, he soon learned that, in the film industry, experience is key, not where your undergraduate degree came from, or often even that you have one. He had assumed he would graduate from school and soon become a hot young director. But instead of jumping into his desired profession to gain experience and work his way up the ladder, he convinced himself that the next logical step was to get a master's degree.

But Charles just couldn't decide what school to apply to, or exactly what part of the film industry he was really interested in, so while he was deciding, he started taking what he termed "McJobs." He was a cab driver; he sold jeans in a mall and insurance door-to-door; he worked in ski shops, bakeries, and every imaginable place that had nothing to do with film, while he contemplated his next move.

Months stretched into years and finally into a decade, and now almost fifteen years later, Charles has yet to make a move toward his declared profession. Embarrassed by the fact that he is a thirty-six-year-old waiter, when people ask what he does, he declares he is a "filmmaker" (explaining, of course, that he is just waiting for his big break). He fails to explain to people that the closest he has come to filmmaking was when he sold popcorn at the Metroplex.

Had Charles just jumped into his desired industry, started at the bottom, and worked toward his goal, he might be where he wants to be now. But instead, he prefers to work his McJobs and contemplate how *the world* has failed *him*.

What Causes Analysis Paralysis. The root of "analysis paralysis" is always fear of failure, but failure is only inevitable if one fails to take action that could potentially lead to success. Subconsciously, Will probably likes to cling to his dream of a successful career in film, but he knows that if he actually takes action toward achieving this goal, one of the potential outcomes is that, for a variety of reasons, he might not succeed, and perhaps he will be forced to abandon his dream.

What Charles refuses to accept is that, in his current scenario, he has adopted the worst of all situations. Perhaps he could be successful as a filmmaker, but he will never really know. Or perhaps he could enjoy a successful and happy career as a waiter, or a restaurant manager, or in one of the many other professions he has "dabbled in" without giving them his full attention, because of his professed goal to work in the film industry. The ultimate result of Charles's lack of action has been to transform him into another Whiner, lamenting about the fact that he has never been able to achieve his goals.

RULE #5: ENJOY THE RIDE: YOU HAVE ONLY ONE LIFE TO LIVE

If you learn only one lesson from this book, perhaps this should be the one. The major attribute that Whiners and Weasels share is *unhappiness*. Unfortunately, it is also a condition that affects a fair percentage of Warriors and Workers and all of those in between. And perhaps most sadly, millions of people are unhappy not because of any *real* condition in their lives that warrants their sadness, but just because they can't allow themselves to enjoy the ride. Their minds won't allow them to enjoy the obvious fruits of their labors that surround them. Instead, they feel needless tension and angst. They might not necessarily be whining about their situation, but they still live their lives lacking the enjoyment they could be experiencing.

I battle this condition myself all the time. Sometimes, I have to mentally slap myself when I realize I'm unduly depressed over inconsequential business problems, a stain on my tie, bad service at a store, or a new door ding on my car. I have to remind myself that I'm healthy and successful, with a beautiful wife and family and every possible option in front of me. It is easy to get overrun with the complications and distractions of life, to the point that you don't realize how wonderful things really are. Many Whiners could find happiness just by realigning their attitude.

"Don't pay the toll twice" is also a good lesson in life. Certainly, it is important to seriously confront life's problems and challenges, but once they are properly addressed, there is no reason to let these issues control one's life.

Live for Today. It's an extremely common human condition to "miss the moment." How many of us have looked back fondly at younger days, perhaps childhood, high school, or college, when things seemed so much simpler and life so much more enjoyable? But in truth, if memory serves me correctly, during those halcyon periods, I—like most people—was looking forward to the future, without full appreciation of what was going on *at that moment.* I dreamt of the freedom of a job and the ability to travel, meet new people, and tackle fresh challenges. And I am sure that I have simply forgotten the problems and hassles of those earlier times. I think we all have to consider the possibility that right now we are living in "the good old days" of the future, and the key is to enjoy them.

And although I am a big proponent of proper planning and control of one's life, rewarding yourself (by maintaining your guidepost and reward tools) makes life worth living. Taking constant inventory of all the good in your life keeps things in perspective, and with an optimistic and realistic viewpoint of your life, you probably won't feel the need to whine.

And Plan for Tomorrow. Although I advocate enjoying the moment, it is essential not to create *future anxiety* by *spending tomorrow's resources today*. It is certainly possible to plan for the future without putting aside the enjoyment one can experience on a daily basis.

For example, if you are a parent, it is important to not only do a Whiner check on yourself, but also to be sure you are not somehow empowering your children to become Whiners. Society is currently primed to create a generation of young complainers who don't want to take responsibility for their own actions.

The best training method to avoid this is by example. If you disdain constant complaining and excuses, your children will pick up on your cue. But it is essential to point out when their petty gossiping, complaining, or negativity goes beyond the bounds of normal conversation into a more dangerous territory. If you allow your children to make excuses for their poor performance and to blame others for what goes wrong in their lives, it will be a lesson to them that whining is acceptable, which leads to all kinds of unfortunate consequences. They should be taught to use their Warrior's tools and to also understand the five rules described in this chapter.

• • • • • • • • • • •

In the next chapter, we will analyze another "Recipe for Failure"
that can lead to Whiner or Weasel behavior.

CHAPTER 16

A Recipe for Failure: "The Procrastinator" Creates More Work—For Everyone

---

"The key is not the 'will to win' ... everybody has that.
It is the will to prepare to win that is important."
—Bobby Knight

N othing comes easier than doing nothing. The fact is we all procrastinate sometimes, and hopefully, some occasional procrastination isn't really all that harmful. It can be a bit therapeutic to Warriors or Workers, providing a little break from their hard work, like one of the coveted "snow days" from your childhood. But we have all probably experienced the occasional and sometimes long-term pain that putting off the inevitable can cause.

RUMINATIONS FROM AN EX-PROCRASTINATOR

I was a terrible procrastinator during my school years. When studying those subjects for which I felt little love or confidence in my ability to master, I justified putting off studying until the last possible minute. At the time, I didn't realize the implications of this procrastination. I was a mediocre student in those subjects I avoided studying, which dragged down my otherwise strong GPA, which made getting into some of my choice colleges impossible.

As a result, I did not meet and befriend Bill Gates at Harvard. Accordingly, the two of us did not form a partnership to develop a computer operating system far superior to anything ever introduced. We did not start Microsoft, and I did not become one of the richest men in the world. This prevented me from establishing the O'Leary Charitable Trust with a billion-dollar donation, which would have funded a cure for AIDS, and saved millions of lives, for which I would have been awarded the Nobel Peace Prize. And all because I put off studying algebra!

Okay, that example might be a bit of a stretch. But although I am certainly not complaining about how things turned out, my early procrastination did create limitations to overcome later in life. In retrospect, I wish that I had applied a little extra effort to certain academic pursuits that would have opened up new worlds to me. Perhaps I still would have chosen the path I did, but I always like to have every possible option open to me.

Occasionally, monitoring your own "procrastinating habits" is a valuable exercise. If putting things off a little is a valid form of relaxation for you, and there is no longer-term price to pay, then it should probably not be of concern. However, if your procrastination is causing you trouble in your life now, it will probably only get worse, and it should be addressed. Given the fact that time is limited for all of us, we all have to choose the most efficient use of our time, but I am often confronted with relatives, employees, and friends who allow their own procrastination to rule their lives.

Of course, some would say procrastination is simply a more charitable term for laziness, which is sometimes the case, but many of the procrastinators I know are not necessarily lazy individuals. In fact, putting off the inevitable often just creates *more work* for them, which they end up doing anyway. And sometimes, the roots of your procrastination need to be examined, as they might reveal some other issue that needs to be addressed.

PROCRASTINATION OFTEN CREATES A MESS

Years ago a friend decided to remodel the exterior of his house. Since he had some background as a contractor (or at least believed he was a handy), he decided to do the work himself. He tore off the siding from the back of his home, installed new windows, and tacked up black liner to the exterior walls in anticipation of reinstalling the siding.

Unfortunately, for some reason he never got around to putting the siding back up. A decade later, the back of his house looks as if Katrina just came knocking. My friend is financially successful and could certainly afford to have the job professionally finished. Instead, he continues to say, "I'm going to finish it next month," and next month never comes.

This goes far beyond normal procrastination (perhaps indicating some psychological hatred of siding), but the idea that he would put up with the discomfort of living that way continues to amaze me. At some point he will most likely sell the house, which will necessitate finishing the job anyway, so there is no real economic gain to his ongoing discomfort.

PROCRASTINATION OFTEN LEADS TO MORE WORK IN THE END

A much more common example of procrastination is a situation I recently faced with a former employee who was a bright young guy. A big part of his job was putting together new client presentations, which unfortunately can often be time-consuming and tedious work, but it's still one of the most important functions in the company. Because many of the components of the presentations are the same regardless of who we are presenting to, it is also a process that could be made extremely efficient by planning ahead and building "modular components" to the presentations that would look better and take less customization. Because our business tends to fluctuate up and down, this person had plenty of "down time" when he could have prepared these components at a reasonable pace.

But no matter how many times I urged the employee to do this, he seemed incapable of taking those steps. Instead, he procrastinated, wasting much of the available time when we were not busy, and instead forcing himself to work long hours right before a presentation was due. He reminded me of myself during my college years, putting off the tough studying when I had the time, and instead, cramming at the last minute.

CURING PROCRASTINATION REQUIRES DISCIPLINE

Staying on top of the tough and tedious duties is difficult, but in the long run, it provides tremendous payoff. I begin every day with a clearly defined set of tasks, and I force myself to tackle the least appealing on a regular basis so they don't overcome me. These tasks may range from the simply mundane I don't feel like doing—to the more dreaded that will be stressful to undertake.

It is particularly easy to procrastinate on the really tough tasks. Nobody likes to fire someone, or make that call with bad news to a client or loved one. But delaying the inevitable just prolongs the pain, and it often threatens your stability. The pain of the task is almost always better than the continued stress of knowing something is looming in front of you. Ultimately, I have found few true procrastinators among the very successful I have encountered.

• • • • • • • • • • • •

In the next section, part 5, we begin our exploration of the dark side, namely the slimy world of Weasels.

PART FIVE

Weasels—How to Not Become One
(Or Reform!)
And How to Get Rid of Them

CHAPTER 17

Sneaky, Beady-Eyed Little Critters: Recognizing Weasel Behaviors and Traits

"The only thing necessary for the triumph of evil is
for good men to do nothing."
—Edmund Burke
(eighteenth century British statesman and orator)

B
ecause I am by no means an expert on animal husbandry, I must
begin this chapter with cautious apologies to the Weasel. I suspect
that the real rodent is probably less heinously regarded in the animal kingdom than the human equivalent that we have tagged with the
moniker.

But like it or not, the human Weasel has certainly become synonymous
in our society with all kinds of bad and untrustworthy personality attributes.
The media portrays them as sneaky, beady-eyed little critters; sociopaths
who put on a positive face and demeanor to trick us, while they plot to
destroy everyone around them for any possible kind of personal gain. They
lie and cheat with wild abandon, sometimes just for the sport of it all.

Their motivations in life seem to range from pure greed to the incomprehensible joy many of them receive when others around them are degraded, miserable, or unsuccessful—especially when they have had a hand in creating the unhappiness.

Weasels regard life as a game that, from their perspective, can only have one winner, and winning means that everyone but them must lose. They often have the ability to evoke a strange kind of pity from those around them, because during intimate moments, they sometimes exhibit a kind of compelling and lonely hollowness that some people find attractive or mysterious, often evoking an almost maternal or paternal instinct from those around them.

But this makes them all the more dangerous, because pity for a Weasel is always misplaced. In the end, they will always manipulate the goodwill that anybody offers them to their own advantage, eventually chewing up and spitting out their friends, coworkers, and business associates when it brings them any kind of benefit or ego boost.

THE NUMBER OF TRULY DESTRUCTIVE WEASELS IS INCREASING

Since I started writing this book, I've noticed that, as a culture, we have recently been confronted with an abundance of particularly heinous Weasels operating on a large scale. They range from the white-collar thugs who ran Enron and WorldCom and robbed thousands of unsuspecting people of their life savings while pillaging their companies, to the most dangerous kind of Weasels who periodically rise to haunt mankind – namely, the terrorists who killed thousands of people on September 11th and who continue to plague the world by killing innocent people in the name of fanaticism.

Although I would never dare equate the run-of-the-mill nasty folks each of us may encounter in our daily lives with the kind of individuals who randomly slaughter innocent people, both are Weasels of different degrees. History is filled with the unfortunate rise of social, religious, political, and military Weasels—individuals and groups who cause tremendous pain to the masses and who temporarily stall society in its tracks, as we all attempt to deal with actions that are almost impossible for us to comprehend. Instead of channeling their energies to change the problems they complain about, they instead focus on harming others in retribution.

In their fanaticism, they exhibit typical cowardly Weasel tendencies, although on a much larger and more dangerous scale than the con men and creeps that we more commonly encounter. They are blind to the concerns of others, and they justify any action they may decide to take. They whine about the injustice they perceive is heaped on them, and they use it to explain their immoral and criminal behavior. Yet despite their pontifications, they refuse to take responsibility for the havoc they wreak.

As Americans, we have been raised to loudly proclaim the superiority of our political system over less free and forthcoming governments, which made the terrorists' actions all the more baffling. They feel strongly enough about their cause that they commit suicide while murdering thousands, seemingly with no regret, yet they are so cowardly that they refuse to publicly acknowledge their actions. Although the atrocities of other groups and governments are not often more tolerable, as a culture, we at least find it more palatable to have enemies who have the courage of their convictions to publicly identify themselves.

Weasels mask their dubious actions with some larger cause—frequently religious or some kind of moral positioning—but in the end, it is always their greed and desire to dominate others and fill the hollowness that drives them. Whether they are mass murderers of Hitler's or the terrorists' ilk or simply common thieves who use their talents to steal from the unsuspecting, Weasels are able to justify any means to fill the gaping hole that exists in their souls. How sad that they don't channel their considerable energies and devotion into effecting *positive* change for their people, as opposed to simply trying to *destroy* those who have been more successful at perfecting their culture.

TYPICAL WEASEL TRAITS, MOTIVATIONS, AND BEHAVIORS

Although they may sometimes appear to be popular, Weasels are loners in the most profound sense, usually trusting no one because they know that they personally can never be trusted, which makes the idea that they could put their faith in anyone else simply incomprehensible. And because their only "friends" are ultimately also Weasels, real lasting friendships become impossible. They simply do not possess the sense of goodwill and empathy that are a part of most people's basic genetic code. Perhaps that is the biggest challenge in dealing with a Weasel. Their souls are so empty or rotten that they cannot comprehend anyone else really feels differently than they do.

Weasels assume everyone shares their same self-serving motivations in life, a "screw-or-be-screwed" attitude. If they were not so damaging to all around them, they would really be sad characters.

Their motivations are baffling to most people; hence, they are especially dangerous, because non-Weasels are hard-pressed to guess a Weasel's next move. Unlike their animal counterpart that is driven by the desire for food, shelter, and other normal instinctual behaviors, human Weasels are fulfilling ego-driven desires that would not occur to most people, and so, they are hard to predict. One would imagine that Weasels seeking money or power would slow down or stop their nefarious activities once they achieve their goals, but the problem is that Weasels never really get what they are after.

For example, most of us would have been satisfied to build assets worth hundreds of millions or billions of dollars and run a quality company. But that was just not enough for the Enron executives. They preferred to turn the company into a massive Ponzi scheme, and finally rob their own workers to make a few more bucks that they could never foresee ably even spending in their lifetimes.

Consider a world-class Weasel like Richard Nixon. One would assume that, after he achieves his lifelong goal of winning and occupying the most important and powerful job in the world, he could kick back his ambitions a bit and concentrate on achieving a few positive goals and perhaps leave a positive legacy. Or at the very least relax and enjoy his achievements and the obvious perks of the position. But a Weasel's mind does not work that way, and consequently, Nixon spent his time destroying his perceived enemies, attempting to extend the Vietnam War, and authorizing common low-life burglaries—all behaviors that are simply baffling to a normal human being.

Because of this personality attribute, a Weasel cannot comprehend "win/win" situations in life or business. To be successful in personal and business relationships, I have always found that developing "win/win" scenarios in any negotiation or conflict should always be the goal to achieve maximum success and certainly harmony. But, to the Weasel, the opposing party in any negotiation or conflict must always be left unhappy and feeling unsuccessful.

Weasel behavior and morals can certainly be taught, and Weasel parents have a much higher probability of creating Weasel offspring by example. Like many of the Whiners discussed earlier in previous chapters, although they certainly can be moronic rednecks who prefer to live their lives as low-life reprobates, petty criminals, and thieves, Weasels are by no means confined to any particular social class. In fact, they are frequently a talented and motivated lot who simply choose to use their talents to foster negativity.

Although we love to watch them as television and movie villains, the problem is that their entertainment persona is unfortunately not that exaggerated from how Weasels live and exist in real life. For example, Mr. Burns from *The Simpsons* is entertaining as an animated character, but there are a lot of real-life "Mr. Burns" actually preying on people every day. Okay, maybe there aren't a large number of Weasels that own nuclear power plants (thank God), but you get the idea. We all know a Weasel or two, and almost all of us have a sad story about an unfortunate run-in with one or more of them.

WEASELS CROP UP IN ALL WALKS OF LIFE

Weasels permeate every segment of society, building mistrust and degrading their lifestyles, professions, families, and social circles as they make their way through life. Their negative impact reaches far beyond the nasty activities in which they partake. In fact, society is constantly forced to construct massive and costly programs to deal with the enormous damage caused by Weasels. They are the bane of our existence; a massive societal parasite that forces us to maintain a cumbersome and expensive military as well as surveillance, treatment, legal, and political systems to assure the malady is kept in check. Weasels subvert our social systems, manipulating the safeguards we build in for everyone's protection for their own benefit.

Although we would certainly always need police forces, courts, and armies to deal with life's normal conflicts, imagine how much smaller and less expensive to maintain these institutions could be if most of their resources were not taken up dealing with Weasels—ranging from career criminals to white-collar criminals to history's most famous Weasels: Hitler, Stalin, Mao, and now the new breed of terrorists who threaten mankind and wreak havoc on all of us. Imagine if the energy we collectively are forced to exert for Weasel protection could instead be used for *positive* social programs! Weasels may very well be one of the main blockades to building the near-utopian society.

Weasel Politicians. As one moves up the social ladder, the many once-proud professions that are now frequently bastions of Weasels have had their integrity and reputations decimated. Study American history and our forefathers, and I guarantee you will come away with a new appreciation for the American system of government, and be filled with intense admiration for the high standards, ethics, and lofty ambitions our political system was built upon.

Unfortunately, this admiration does not extend to many of today's politicians. Although I am confident that a high percentage of those in public service are there with the same admirable motivations of a Washington or Jefferson, Weasels have unfortunately been attracted to the power and prestige of our governing bodies, forcing most Americans to regard politicians with the same esteem normally reserved for used-car salesmen and screaming purveyors of imported rugs. Instead of serving the public, they choose to serve personal agendas that often tear the country apart. The saddest consequence of this situation is that with its image tarnished, public service no longer attracts the fine candidates that would once find it an admirable profession, leaving more room for Weasels to flourish—and for the rest of us to pay the price.

IDENTIFYING TYPICAL WEASEL TRAITS

The fact that Weasels frequently become financially successful compounds the problem. Unfortunately, for society to work properly, we need a system that to a certain extent rewards aggression on many fronts, and Weasels (like all Warriors) are frequently aggressive. The irony of the situation is that although Weasels might believe they do their dastardly deeds for the money or fame, the truth is that, ultimately, they don't discover satisfaction in either. They are parasites that keep feeding on others, but they never manage to fill up the gaping hole inside them, which in most people is occupied by a soul.

This is ultimately what separates a Weasel from an individual who might have a good heart but is morally challenged. The morally challenged—even the morally decrepit—sometimes see the error of their ways and reform. Although they are driven by ego and greed, they maintain some sense of concern for others. The true Weasel almost never changes his or her colors and almost always exhibits the traits described in the following sections (if they ever allow you to dig deep enough to reveal any of their personality).

Weasels Are Insecure. Because insecurity is perhaps one of the most common universal personality attributes we almost all share (hence the earlier chapter completely devoted to the condition), it is not surprising that Weasels exhibit this trait. And certainly, being insecure does not make you a Weasel. However, whether or not they show it to those around them, Weasels' sense of insecurity reaches heights a normal human being cannot imagine, and it essentially defines them. It festers from simple self-doubt to full-blown constant feelings of inadequacy, finally mutating to an often-internalized but dangerous anger and hatred of anyone who is higher on the food chain than they are. This attitude and emotion is what gives Weasels a perceived carte blanche to do whatever is necessary to further their own goals, regardless of the impact on anyone around them. It ultimately becomes the defining emotion of the Weasel.

Although many of us may be haunted by feelings of insecurity, the majority of people learn to deal with it and find joy in their lives through their own accomplishments, the accomplishments of those around them, and the friendship and fellowship of others. However, Weasels take that insecurity and turn it to hate: their perverse reason for living. This is what leads them to experience joy in the failure of others. They revel in the idea that another's problems may cause them to feel more insecure and unhappy than the Weasels do. They perceive that the failures or unhappiness of others signal success for them.

Accordingly, they will take pride in building relationships that most would cherish, but Weasels will destroy with no remorse, because it gives them a feeling of superiority that feeds their egos.

Certainly managing insecurity is a battle most of us fight, and as covered in chapter 8, it can be a recipe for failure. But if your insecurities are causing you to take constant joy in the pain of others, you are a Weasel-on-the-cusp or you have already made the transition.

Weasels Are Completely Self-Obsessed. Although Weasels may pretend to exhibit generous traits, it is essential to realize that they are completely preoccupied with themselves: they are functional sociopaths focused on their own needs. Any sign of generosity, compassion, or love to another masks their true motivation, which always revolves around achieving a personal goal that feeds their endless hollow pit of insecurity.

Certainly, not every self-obsessed or insecure person is a Weasel (or we would be a society of Weasels), but Weasels reach an entirely new level. They will discard friends, family, and loved ones for personal gain without another thought. And their feelings of jealousy and competition, even with family and friends, are so intense that they can share no pride or joy in others' accomplishments.

I find a little self-analysis in the area is often valuable. It's a good idea to periodically check yourself for creeping signs of Weasel behavior. Allowing yourself to take tiny steps into the world of Weasels can sometime lead to disaster.

Weasels Lack Self-responsibility. Most Weasels are masters of the excuse. If they fail to perform in any aspect of their lives, it is never through any fault of their own. Instead, they are experts at the "blame game," and they often use this technique quite successfully to maneuver through their lives. This lacking also makes it relatively simple for Weasels to abandon the seemingly most important people in their lives. Most of us would find it incomprehensible that a father or mother could walk out on their spouse and family, often abandoning them with no contact for years, decades, or even a lifetime, but the Weasels who do this somehow find justification. In the workplace, a Weasel always has an excuse if cornered for poor performance (and that usually involves pinning the blame on someone else).

Again, periodic self-analysis and the gumption to accept responsibility are essential to keep this trait from overrunning you. Warriors take responsibility. While I will certainly analyze the situations and the Weasels that led to my personal and career failures, they were ultimately my own fault. While Weasels may have played a major role in building the problems, I allowed them to happen.

We have all had to observe this Weasel trait firsthand during the recent corporate scandals. High paid CEOs whine that the collapse of their business empires were not their fault and they should not be responsible. "It was the finance guys—I had nothing to do with it" is the common refrain. Yet months and years earlier, they were on the front page of the business publications taking credit as the brilliant businesspeople responsible for the company's success.

Managers also need to be on the watch for these traits so they can either properly train the employee to take responsibility for their actions, or get them out of the organization before they do permanent damage.

Weasels Are Unreasonably Competitive. Because Weasels are constantly concentrating on what they don't have, as opposed to what they do possess, they live lives filled with jealousy and unreasonable competitiveness with those around them. And this can be a tough one to judge. Warriors by their very nature are competitive, and you don't want to mistake that trait in yourself or others as a negative attribute.

However, a Warrior will actually have admiration for other Warriors who successfully compete with them. I admire my successful competitors who compete fairly and ethically and (hopefully only occasionally) beat me. They make me and my organization better and improve the marketplace. And if we are all on a level playing field and we lose, it is our problem. And my Warrior competitors feel the same about me, which leads to a competitive, but much more professional and pleasant business environment.

A Weasel never takes any pleasure or learns a lesson from their competitor's success. They will take any advantage—ethical or not—to win the account. They will disparage their competitors at every opportunity. They will whine when they lose—and blame everyone but themselves for their lack of success. If you see yourself or your employees slipping into this habit, do a little Weasel housecleaning right away.

Weasels Are Master Politicians. I am not specifically referring to the numerous Weasels who unfortunately populate government, but rather the fact that many Weasels are much more politically attuned than the average individual. They typically grasp the power structure of an organization faster than most, and they immediately begin to use it to their advantage. Because they are particularly attuned to their own insecurities, they "dial in" on individual and organizational insecurities and begin to manipulate these weaknesses to their advantage. They are especially effective at appearing to be supportive, while at the same time fostering instability. Weasels will be their supervisor's biggest advocate publicly, while planting the seeds of discontent with the boss's boss so they gleefully eliminate the supervisor on their way up the ladder.

To effectively guard against this kind of Weasel infestation, you need to first do a little analysis of those around you. Could a Weasel have possible worked his or her way into your inner circle and gained your trust, which ultimately he or she plans to use against you? Employees who are behaving in a Weasel-like manner against their fellow employees might not pose a threat to you right now, but ultimately, they will set their sights on your job, so it is best to shut them down early. Weasels also will play to your ego to gain your confidence, so you need to be wary of someone else's ego pumping to make sure it is genuine.

Weasels Are Consummate Actors. The ability to put on a "false face" is certainly a valuable talent Weasels use constantly. As they maneuver their way through life, they typically have the ability to be different things to different people, until they eventually show their true colors.

One of the most frequent acting talents I have observed among most Weasels is the ability to mask their innate laziness. They typically have the ability to look incredibly busy doing important work, but once really pinned down, they are really accomplishing very little. Beware of the employees or coworkers who spend inordinate amounts of time talking about how hard they work (a Whiner and a Warrior trait), as they are usually the ones hardly working.

• • • • • • • • • • • •

In the next chapter, we'll look at ways to develop "Weasel Radar."

CHAPTER 18

Weasels at Work — and How to Develop "Weasel Radar"

The Ballad of Les the Weasel
(Sung to the tune of "The Beverly Hillbillies")
"Tell ya' a little story bout' a man named Les,
Put your trust in him, and he'll make a great big mess,
Acts like a preacher, while he squanders all the cash,
Robbed all his friends so he could throw a great big bash,
Swimming pools, hotel suites, workin' girls . . ."

O kay, so I probably shouldn't abandon my day job for a career as a songwriter, but over twenty years after my encounter with Les, one of my first major Weasel run-ins as a businessman, I at least have a sense of humor about our relationship. And as much as I wish I had never met him, he helped me begin to develop the Weasel radar that has ultimately helped me avoid much more serious collisions with much smarter and considerably more menacing Weasels.

WHY IT'S SO DIFFICULT TO SPOT WEASELS RIGHT AWAY

The problem for non-Weasels is actually imagining the sociopath mindset of the Weasel. To develop good Weasel radar, a normal person needs to completely alter his or her understanding of human motivation. It would not occur to most of us to destroy the good things in our lives simply to feed our egos, but to Weasels, this makes complete sense, because they are ruled by a completely different set of priorities. The concepts of honor, friendship, respect built on respecting others, and even the normal desires for financial success and security take a backseat to ego pumping that goes far beyond a normal human being's imagination. The concept of win/win does not occur to Weasels: they simply can't regard a situation turning out successfully unless someone loses.

And even when discovered, a true Weasel feels none of the guilt or remorse that plague normal people when they are caught doing wrong. Ultimately, this is what truly separates the Weasel from those who were temporarily morally challenged. We all have many acts in our past that we are not proud of—whether we were caught, or we simply suffered the consequences of our dishonesty in private. But the act of regret and suffering—in whatever form we experience those emotions—is what separates a normal human from a Weasel.

Instead of feeling the necessary remorse, Weasels simply concentrate on filling the emptiness they feel inside—an emptiness that never goes away, no matter how much they feed it. They become oblivious to the plight of others, unless recognizing that plight somehow benefits them. Many of the more talented Weasels mask their emptiness for long periods, becoming successful and well regarded, but at some point, their lack of self-respect spews out, often infecting or damaging everyone around them.

Luckily, once you begin to comprehend how they operate, Weasels do tend to make predictable moves and operate in similar fashions, which makes developing Weasel radar possible. Most of the successful people I have encountered have finely tuned Weasel radar. It's a pity I didn't have those tools before being introduced to Les.

MY FIRST MAJOR WEASEL ENCOUNTER—AND THE LESSONS I LEARNED

I met Leslie when I launched my first serious enterprise, a software company I founded in the early 1980s. I was an arrogant twenty-two-year-old with an overinflated opinion of my business acumen (which, at that point, was purely based on theory with no practical experience). This very scenario made me a good target for Leslie, and she was quick to gain my confidence by telling me all kinds of wonderful (but mostly unjustified) things about myself.

I was filled with a Warrior's aggression and a few useful tools, and I occasionally did have good ideas. The company I started was ahead of its time, had tremendous potential, and was poised for fast growth. Given the fact that I was young, inexperienced, frequently stupid, and more a marketer than a programmer or technical type, I needed a "talented and honest geek" to help me build the company.

A friend referred me to Leslie, and I was immediately impressed by her technical qualifications and overall presence. She had the personality of a conservative but kind aunt, and from the beginning we hit it off. She seemed extremely intelligent and levelheaded, and her very demeanor inspired trust. I was sure I had found the key person who would help the company succeed.

In fact, our relationship transcended just business; she became my confidante at work and, like the big sister I never had, in life, too.

And the relationship was extremely beneficial to both of us. The new position meant considerably more money, a vice president's title, potential equity in a growing company, and an exciting future. I have never been a micro-manager, and I also gave Leslie great latitude in how she ran her department. She managed all the technical operations and had an enormous amount of contact with our clients. That was my first mistake.

Beware of Giving Too Much Control to People You Don't Really Know. Because I was busy with the day-to-day strategic, marketing, and financial operations of the company (and given my lack of technical expertise), I allowed Leslie to take complete control of the technical side of the business, which is really the heart and soul of a software company. She hired and managed the staff, she trained new distributors on the operations of the system, she set policy and the development path, and I had little interaction with the most important part of the company.

Although we were reasonably successful from the onset, I had no experience properly funding a start-up operation. Despite our growing business, we were rapidly running out of cash, which started me on the difficult and time-consuming road to money raising. However, I felt great about the fact that my valued right-hand woman and good friend Leslie was keeping an eye on the company. And Leslie reinforced my attitude, frequently telling me how I could always trust her and how devoted she was to the vision of the company. (A common Weasel action: they often overemphasize how honest and trustworthy they are, while they plan for your demise.)

But that all changed when I happened to run into one of my programmers having a drink one night in a bar near our office. Perhaps fueled by the fact that he had been in the bar for at least an hour before I arrived, the programmer told me a disturbing story about Leslie .

"The lady hates you," he said matter-of-factly, "and she is constantly talking to the staff about how she is the brains of the operation and you are just a punk kid who got lucky and will blow all the company's money. She says she is going to find a way to get rid of you, and soon."

Check Out Weasel-Like Behavior. After my conversation with the programmer, I did some intensive investigation. I discovered, much to my dismay, that he was not only telling the truth, but that my friend Leslie had a dark side I was completely unaware of.

Get Rid of Weasels as Soon as You Can. When I confronted Leslie, she denied the allegations, even when presented with irrefutable proof. And because I had trusted her so completely and allowed her to take such a predominant role in the company, I was in a terrible situation. I determined that I could not just fire her—as she held the keys to so much information and client relationships. Ultimately, getting away from her while keeping the company intact became my primary objective. Ultimately, I sold the company to her.

If I had been more experienced in the ways of Weasels, I would have discovered Leslie much earlier, and I would have dealt with her much more effectively. But due to my inexperience, I simply ejected her from my office and did my best to clean up the mess.

In later years, when I would encounter her, she would smile and wave and act as if nothing had ever transpired between us. Weasels feel no guilt over their actions.

Weasel Post-Mortem. Had Leslie concentrated on *succeeding* at the tasks in front of her and been a team player instead of letting her Weasel ways rule her actions, we both would have enormously profited from the relationship. But I need to take most of the blame for what happened. As the boss, it was my job to Weasel-proof the company for everyone's good, and I failed at my task. In retrospect I should have:

- Kept my ego in check. I allowed a Weasel to pump my ego and gain my trust through my own arrogance.

- Checked Leslie out much more completely. I trusted her before she had earned it. Weasels usually leave a slimy trail, so it is essential to do a thorough background check on someone.

- Taken the time to understand the very heart of my business; because I didn't, this allowed someone else to take control.

- Not have continued to do business with a Weasel. Once discovered, I should have found a way to completely eliminate Leslie from the equation while minimizing the impact to the company. I should have been much smarter in my planning, instead of panicking and taking the easier path of selling the company to her, which actually ended up costing me more money and heartache.

- Hired a couple of strong-armed gentlemen to take Leslie out in the desert and bury her. (Wait—just kidding—nix that idea. Although that's what I might have fantasized about doing, you need to take your satisfaction in the fact that Weasels always end up paying the price for their rodent ways.)

As I have stated throughout this book, dealing with a Weasel is similar to dealing with a physical disease. Early detection is the key. And after I understood Leslie's true colors, it was idiotic of me to continue to deal with her and in fact sell her the company without full payment upfront. If you continue to trust a Weasel, you get what you deserve.

WHAT ELSE DO WEASELS DO?

- Weasels create conflict and dissension.

- Weasels build allies inside and outside the operation.

- Weasels put on a happy face.

- Weasels feed the rumor mill.

- Weasels establish a scapegoat.

- Weasels take the fun out of life.

- Weasels try to pass themselves off as saviors.

- Weasels destroy the evidence and rewrite history.

- Weasels then move on to the next victim.

HOW TO SPOT A WEASEL: MORE SIGNS TO WATCH FOR

In addition to the major Weasel actions listed above, the rest of this chapter describes a few additional indicators that should at least sound a preliminary ring of your Weasel radar. Although exhibiting one or two of the attributes (or utilizing a classic Weasel excuse) does not automatically qualify someone for Weasel status, it should put you on guard (or perhaps give you reason to confront them before their Weasel behavior spreads).

Also, do a little self-analysis to see if you unconsciously exhibit any of these Weasel traits. It occasionally happens to all of us, and a little personal tune-up couldn't hurt.

The "Too Bad I Didn't Get There Earlier" Excuse. Most of the Weasels I have encountered are filled with excuses about their earlier lack of success, and these excuses usually revolve around them coming into the situation a little too late to be able to save the day. I say "lack of success," because most Weasels would never actually admit to "failing" at anything. More typically, they have an excuse for something that occurred earlier in their career that has hampered them, and this excuse usually involves someone else's incompetence.

For example, when I initially hired Les and queried him about his failed business enterprise, he blamed the failure on the person who had owned the company before him. "I thought I could turn it around, but I just got there a little too late to save it," he expressed sadly. "The previous owner had just driven it too far into the ground."

This sign is often a bit tough to read, because I have found that people who have tried, failed, and learned from their failure are typically in a better position to be successful the next time around. But the difference between an honest person and a Weasel is that the honest person will readily admit the mistake he or she made, as opposed to placing all the blame elsewhere.

Weasels in romantic relationships also play their own version of this game. Past relationships didn't work out because their partner was "crazy" or "jaded" before they got there. "I really thought I could help her (or him), but she was really too far gone, and so we didn't work out," they sadly lament, failing to mention their enormous contribution to destroying the relationship.

In a job interview, I now look for certain signs that would indicate this Weasel tendency. Unless an applicant specializes in being a turnaround specialist, it is highly unusual to meet people who have had a series of jobs, all at companies that went out of business, so if I run into this I do a much more extensive background check on the individual.

The Real Problem Is that "You Are Crazy" Excuse. Another common and highly effective Weasel technique is to attempt to get others to feel as if they have a problem. Individuals in relationships with Weasels commonly suffer this attack. Weasels frequently target the emotionally weak or those who tend to spend a lot of time self-analyzing, because they are easy marks. They are masters at homing in on someone else's insecurities or vulnerable points, and with this knowledge in hand, they begin to subtly chip away, often finally blowing up these insecurities to use as a devastating tool against their targets.

Weasels in the workplace will also attempt to keep coworkers (and even their superiors) off guard by feeding their self-doubts. Weasels will sometimes even offer their counseling assistance to help their "friend" work through his or her problems, which gives Weasels ample opportunity to learn more about weak points and to keep heaping on reasons for insecurity. It is an easy and effective way to gain the upper hand.

To counter this technique, you need to stay firm in your convictions, stay guarded until you are sure you can trust those whom you would take into your confidence, and keep your self-confidence up.

Pity the Seemingly Hard-Working Weasel. Weasels are typically quite good at creating the *illusion* of activity—even though, in reality, they are usually just wasting time. They are always quick to point out how hard they do work or how difficult their life is, in an attempt to either garner pity or respect, which they will turn into a weapon at a later date.

They commonly use the "hard work" excuse throughout their day-to-day lives at work and at home. "I didn't call the client back because I was working round the clock on the secret report." Or, "I didn't have time to get you a birthday gift because I was working those long hours just to keep food on the table." Weasels will say anything to avoid the real issue and to make themselves martyrs.

I find that Warriors and Workers don't make excuses—it is a Whiner or Weasel reaction. Although the Warrior or Worker might legitimately be overworked, they know that it is not an excuse not to get the job done. Rather, they will request help or make the necessary changes to assure that the job is completed.

The Weasel's Sense of Entitlement. Weasels tend to have an ingrained sense of entitlement that extends to all levels of their existence. Not only does the world owe them something, but virtually everyone they come in contact with does, too. This is an easy trait to spot and luckily will sometimes reveal the Weasel early in the game.

Weasels Deny Anything and Everything. When confronted about anything potentially damaging, the Weasel has the ability to completely deny responsibility, regardless of the situation. You could literally catch a Weasel naked in bed with your spouse, and when confronted, he or she would stare at you blankly and act as if nothing was wrong. "Quit talking crazy; you know I would never sleep with your wife," the Weasel would insist, as he got dressed and walked out of your bedroom. Again, it points to the importance of having your data gathered and your facts straight when you deal with a Weasel.

Weasels Abandon Personal Responsibility. Usually, most Weasels or Weasels-on-the-cusp begin their descent to the dark side by first abandoning any sense of personal responsibility. Refusing to accept responsibility for your own actions is a slippery road that makes it easy to engage in the full gamut of Weasel actions. Recently, I watched a client make these first disturbing steps.

A FEW STEPS TO WEASEL-PROOF YOUR LIFE

I have discovered that minimizing the impact of Weasels in your life involves a few simple steps that were probably apparent from the case studies above.

- *Check them out.* Unfortunately, once people fall into the Weasel ranks, they seldom seem to change their colors. So one good way to help Weasel-proof your life is to look at someone's history when hiring or associating yourself with someone new. And that research should extend past the normal reference calls. Talk to people who would be intimately familiar with their personal brands, and look for patterns. Certainly, we should all be given the opportunity to redeem ourselves, but past actions do need to be accounted for, and because true Weasels never really feel remorse, they tend to constantly repeat their actions. If you choose to deal with an established Weasel, you ultimately proceed at your own risk.

- *Watch for typical Weasel patterns.* Ego pumping, excuses, gossiping, building dissension and problems where problems did not previously exist, and establishing scapegoats are Weasel techniques you should be aware of.

- *Keep in mind that* your *greed and conceit are a Weasel's best friends.* If you allow yourself to be ego pumped by strangers, or jump at the deal that is "too good to be true," you are opening the door to every Weasel that passes by.

- *Remember that trust is earned, not granted.* It sounds simple, but Weasels count on the fact that via their charm, their manipulation, or even their distortion of the facts, they will gain your trust and access to what they want to steal from you.

- *Trust your instincts.*

- *Make "no Weasels allowed" part of your personal brand.* Weasels typically don't like confrontation; they prefer to work in the shadows. If you are known to have little or no Weasel tolerance, they will move on to an easier mark. And loudly uncovering Weasels is a great service to the next person they might try to take advantage of.

• • • • • • • • • • • •

In the next chapter, you will learn a great new party game, and we'll also review a few of my all-time personal favorite Weasel tales.

CHAPTER 19

The Way of the Weasel: Four of My Favorite Weasel Stories

"Nixon is a shifty-eyed goddamn liar. . . . He's one of the few in the history of this country to run for high office talking out of both sides of his mouth at the same time and lying out of both sides."
— Harry S Truman

Are you searching for a great party game or topic for dinnertime conversation? My suggestion is to play "My Favorite Weasel." Over the years, I have asked friends and associates to tell me their favorite Weasel stories, and I have found most people have some great ones. This chapter describes a few of my favorites.

THE GRAVE-ROBBING WEASEL

About ten years ago, my cousin lost her husband in a tragic accident. While at the mortuary making preparations for the burial, she asked the mortician if she could bury her husband in his favorite cowboy boots. She explained that a year earlier she had the highly unusual, one-of-a-kind boots custom-made for her husband as a special gift, and it would mean a lot to both of them for him to go on to the everlasting with this token of their love. The mortician thought it was a wonderful idea, and he assured her that her husband would be "buried with his boots on."

About a year later, my cousin was walking downtown when she unexpectedly ran into the mortician. He seemed a bit nervous and anxious to get away as they exchanged pleasantries, and when she looked down at his feet, she knew why. The mortician was wearing her dead husband's boots!

Note to Weasels: grave robbing gets you an automatic nomination into the Weasel Hall of Fame.

ROMEO, THE CRYING WEASEL

I heard this story from a woman I met in Vancouver, Canada. A few years earlier, she had fallen in love with a handsome, charming man she met at a fund-raising event. He was a successful architect, and after dating for a year, they became engaged. He explained that as a wedding gift, he was building them a weekend cabin in the woods, and for the next few months, he would be gone on many Saturdays and Sundays, staying in a tent on the property while he constructed their love nest. She at first objected, saying she wanted to be with him, but he insisted that this was a wonderful romantic gesture he wanted to make by himself to start their lives together. "Our little cabin in the woods will be like a monument to our love," he insisted.

One Saturday night, while he was off working at the cabin, she attended another fund-raising event by herself. She was seated next to an attractive woman about her age, and as they conversed, she was pleased to learn this woman was also engaged to be married. The conversation went something like this:

"So what does your fiancée do?" woman #1 inquired.

"He's an architect," said woman #2.

"Wow, what a coincidence, so is mine," she replied enthusiastically. "Maybe they know each other. Where does he work?"

And after hearing the reply, she replied with growing unease, "Wow, what a coincidence, my fiancée works there, too."

I am sure you have guessed the rest. The architect had been engaged to both women for a year. He told woman #2 that he was working on an out-of-town project and could only see her on the weekends, and of course, he used the "most likely fictional cabin love nest" excuse on woman #1.

After expressing their mutual outrage, the two women decided to do a little Weasel confrontation. Woman #1 informed my friend that Romeo Weasel was due to come to her house later that night. (For some reason, he had been unavailable to attend the dinner with her—perhaps there was fiancée #3?) The two women went back to her place to wait, and when he came through the door, they were both calmly sitting in the living room sipping wine.

According to my friend, Romeo Weasel turned white with shock, fell to the ground, pulled himself into a fetal position, and began wailing like a baby. He cried out ridiculous excuses about how he never felt loved and that was why he acted in such a shameful manner.

"He actually did us both a favor by reacting that way," she explained with a laugh, "because as we looked at him, I knew both of us were thinking 'wow, how could we have ever been in love with that?' although we did have to fight the temptation to kick him around the room a bit." Needless to say, Romeo lost two fiancées that night.

WEASELS IN THE FAMILY

There is nothing more disgusting than a Weasel who takes advantage of the disadvantaged—the elderly, the young, the handicapped, and those in need. And unfortunately, there is no lack of such stories—about creeps who deal in human slavery, pedophiles, con men who steal an elderly person's last dollars—the stories go on and on.

But one must really wonder about the kind of Weasel who decides to take advantage of his own elderly grandmother. A fellow passenger on a plane told me about the black-sheep Weasel in his family. His brother, a rather "down-and-out" young man, had taken a renewed interest in visiting their grandmother. Knowing the disreputable character of their brother, the siblings were a bit suspicious, but the elderly woman was so enjoying the attention that they all felt it might be okay.

It was only when the grandmother fell ill that they uncovered what a Weasel their brother really was. The doctor discovered that the creep had been stealing the grandmother's vital medication and replacing it with vitamin pills. When the family did a little more investigation, they found that the thief had also slowly been stealing the old lady's possessions and selling them to buy his own drugs.

THE SPYING WEASEL

Here is one lifted from the pages from the local crime log a few years ago. The owner of a local tanning salon decided to mix a little business with pleasure, so he installed hidden cameras in his tanning rooms. A year or two after the installation, police discovered the cameras and a collection of hundreds of videos he had recorded from the cameras. Because many of the customers were underage girls, Tan Man faced some particularly serious penalties for his voyeurism.

• • • • • • • • • • • •

In the next chapter, we will examine the enormous cost all of us pay due to Weasels, a fee that I like to call the Weasel tax.

# WEASELS

CHAPTER 20

The Weasel Tax:
The High Price We All Pay for
Rodent Infestation

"Expecting life to treat you well because you are a good person
is like expecting an angry bull not to charge
because you are a vegetarian. "

— Shari R. Barr

W
easels are not only annoying and sometimes dangerous, but
they are also incredibly expensive! In fact, we all pay essentially what amounts to a Weasel tax—and this tax is probably
a lot more than most of us imagine, plus it's increasing every year. In fact,
the true cost of Weasels is probably impossible to tabulate, as the Weasel
tax really consists of six components:

1. **Weasel Preventative Costs:** Includes additional insurance; security;
   police and enforcement officials; attorneys; overly complex contracts;
   training time and personnel costs to "Weasel-proof" organizations;
   special Weasel-proofing construction; annoying airport security;

211

expensive protective local, state, and federal agencies specifically aimed at Weasel behavior; huge bumpers to protect your car from drunk Weasels; electronic firewalls and virus protection software; rubber gloves; the list goes on and on.

2. **Weasel Elimination and Isolation Costs:** Includes law enforcement and legal and court fees, payoffs for silly Weasel lawsuits, jails and prisons, penicillin, monitoring costs to make sure Martha Stewart doesn't leave her estate, salaries for worthless Weasels you would like to fire but can't due their litigious nature, etc.

3. **Weasel Theft Costs:** Includes the cost of what Weasels con, steal, and destroy. The massive worthless pork programs that Weasel politicians push through to stay in office and assure their seats on luxury junkets can also be put in this category.

4. **Weasel Loss-of-Productivity Costs:** Includes loss of valuable business time, intellectual and financial capital, and other resources due to Weasels.

5. **Higher Social Costs Due to Weasels:** Includes increased taxes, insurance premiums, governmental costs, construction costs, and many other Weasel-related fees that have to be passed down to consumers and tax payers.

6. **The Weasel Emotional Tax:** Although this is impossible to measure, just think about the stress and hassle we all experience thanks to Weasels.

It's a little difficult to isolate the Weasel tax from costs society would otherwise incur in its day-to-day operations. Certainly, even if there were no Weasels, we would still need infrastructure: police, armies, lawyers, government agencies, disaster insurance, jails for criminals, and many other departments and services. But our societal acceptance of Weasels and the subsequent infestation have run up the bill in many different ways. This chapter offers a few interesting financial statistics to consider.

THE HIGH COST OF PETTY CRIMINALS

Let's start with one of the silliest of crimes that benefits no one—vandalism. At least a thief derives some kind of end benefit by stealing something of value, but vandalism is destruction for destruction's sake—usually carried out by youngsters who are Weasels-in-training. And the cost to Americans every year? *$12 billion.* Yes—that's "billion" with a "B." And vandalism impacts a lot of people compared to most crimes. More than 290,000 people are victims of vandalism every year. In fact, the destruction and defacing of signs alone costs us more than $50 million a year.

Last year, car theft in the United States totaled more than $8.6 billion, and all of us pay the price in higher insurance premiums, with an almost 10 percent average increase in the four-year period between 1998 and 2002. And Weasels steal a lot more than cars. There were more than 7 million additional thefts in the U.S., totaling an additional almost $5 billion in losses.

BUT SERIOUS CRIME IS MUCH MORE EXPENSIVE

Moving way up the scale of seriousness is gun violence. The cost of gun violence in the U.S. runs more than $100 billion a year, and much of it is paid by taxpayers. In fact, each gang murder ends up costing taxpayers more than a million dollars, once all the costs for enforcement and trials are tabulated; when you add in the cost of incarcerating the murderer, that number goes to $1.75 million per gang murder. In Southern California alone, there were more than 3,100 gang murders in the last five years. Over the last fourteen years, King Medical Center alone in Southern California spent $271 million treating gunshot wounds—96 percent of which was paid for with public funds.

And when we do catch these criminals, housing them is the next huge expense. The budget just for the Federal Prison System in 2006 is estimated at $4.8 billion.

WHITE-COLLAR CRIMINALS: THE REALLY EXPENSIVE "REAL" WEASELS

Consider the most recent statistic: *white-collar crime in this country, including workplace fraud, costs $600 billion.*

Certainly, corporations don't bear this financial burden alone. It must be passed down to consumers via higher prices, to workers via lower wages and benefits, and to stockholders via lower performance of their equities. This works out to about $4,500 per worker in this country.

The Weasels who turn a fender bender into a life-changing whiplash economic boon are also taxing all of us. The tab for insurance fraud is more than $80 billion a year, which works out to about $950 for every family in this country.

Healthcare fraud is an even bigger problem, with estimated costs as high as $90 billion per year!

Bankruptcy reform has been a hot topic over the last few months, and with good reason, because *the number of bankruptcies has tripled since 1994.* Bankruptcies currently cost us all about $4 billion a year—which averages out to around $400 to each of us who play the game fairly.

Another hot topic these days is tort reform. The ability to punish corporations for their Weasel ways is an essential tool, but an entirely new breed of Weasel is taking this tool and beating us all over the head with it. Class-action suits that primarily end up lining law firm coffers instead of benefiting plaintiffs have risen 1000 percent in state courts over the last few years, and 300 percent at the federal level. And the total cost of the tort system is $246 billion.

And what would it be like if we all paid our taxes fairly? Abusive tax shelters alone are estimated at $250–$300 billion per year—which works out to a 15 percent surcharge on the average taxpayer who plays by the rules.

THE ADDICT TAX

We all pay the price for those who can't—or refuse—to control themselves. The total social cost of drug abuse in this country has been increasing at 5.9 percent a year for the last decade, and in the most recent tallied year (2002), it topped $181 billion! The federal budget just for the Department of Drug Enforcement is $2.14 billion this year.

Drunk drivers cost us all $45 billion in property damage, and $1.5 billion a year in enforcement and preventative costs.

And we all pay for the guy down the hall who sneaks out for a couple drinks at lunch or a snort in the restroom. Substance abuse in the workplace is estimated at $100 billion a year in lost productivity and increased healthcare costs.

Smokers may lament the high price of cigarettes and the increased cigarette taxes they have to pay—but the rest of us who don't puff should be the ones complaining! Each pack of cigarettes ends up costing all of us an additional $7.18 over the price the smoker paid for the weeds, in increased healthcare costs and lost productivity. And these costs may be a drop in the bucket. Depending on which expert you believe, the estimated cost to society over the next twenty-five years to deal with smoking-related healthcare costs and issues will be somewhere between $50 billion and $1.8 trillion.

Add to these costs the huge amounts we pay to support gambling addicts, the lost productivity and healthcare costs expended to those with eating disorders, and the other wide variety of addiction costs to society, and pretty soon we are talking about some real money.

TECHNOLOGY WEASELS

Along with many interesting innovations, the Internet and the technology boom have also provided fertile breeding ground for an entirely new kind of Weasel—techno rodents.

Most of us are rightfully concerned about identity fraud. In 2004, 9.3 million people had their identities stolen, and the numbers are increasing.

The most despicable Weasels tend to prey on those least able to protect themselves. Last year, the unsuspecting elderly lost more than $52 million to Internet scams. And we paid more than $130 million just to protect ourselves from "PC attacks"—which was probably a good move, because those insidious wasteful viruses that seem to continually circulate cost us all more than $55 billion!

WEASELS WHO STEAL YOUR BODY AND SOUL

In 2005, we still have a problem in America with "human traffickers"— one of the slimiest breeds of Weasels. And the tab we pay? $96 million.

And as one raised in a good Catholic family, I am particularly disturbed about the heinous actions of a few "men of the cloth" who chose to remove their cloths. The cost to date to settle cases for the approximate ten thousand molestation cases currently filed has topped $650 million.

AND THAT'S JUST THE BEGINNING OF WEASEL PROLIFERATION

And this is just a drop in the bucket for the massive tax we all pay to protect ourselves and to pay off and confine Weasels. Think about the enormous and expensive infrastructure we have built and maintain to feel safe from unethical creeps, and the many ways they still manage to dig through our defenses.

Of course, I need to make a clear delineation between Weasels and criminals. Although a Weasel can be and often is a criminal, not all criminals are Weasels. And I would not be foolish enough to suggest that we could completely eliminate crime by just eliminating Weasels. Crimes—and the many motivations of criminals—are virtually impossible to completely eliminate.

WHAT WE COULD BE SPENDING OUR MONEY ON IF NOT FOR WEASELS

It's hard for most of us to comprehend these enormous numbers, but comparing the various Weasel taxes against what we pay for positive programs becomes very illuminating.

Raising Healthy, Smart Kids. As covered throughout this book, simply being smart and/or educated does not automatically prevent you from becoming a Weasel, but populating society with healthy, well-fed kids is our responsibility, and it pays off in many ways. The best way to stamp out Weasel behavior is to start by properly raising our children. Luckily, government sees the wisdom of this and is supporting a lot of programs, but when you compare the expense of these programs against the Weasel tax, the high price we are paying for bad behavior is apparent.

For example, consider the cost of the following programs, as compared to what we have to spend on Weasel taxes:

- The Center for Disease Control's budget to help fight birth defects last year was $124 million, or roughly what we paid just to protect ourselves against PC virus attacks.

- The U.S. Department of Agriculture's WIC program helps feed economically disadvantaged women and their children, and it's especially beneficial to low-income pregnant women. This is a big and important program with a budget of $5.2 billion—but again, this is *approximately one-tenth of the amount we ended up losing to PC viruses.* Hmmm, how does the Weasel mind work? I can either be a good human being, and accordingly feed ten times more poor pregnant women and their kids and hopefully create a better society, or I can express my hatred for Microsoft and society by sending out a virus called "Hello From Your Sister" that destroys the Outlook files of people I have never met. Naturally, Weasels choose the latter.

● Head Start is also a terrific program that assists with childcare development and other services for pregnant women and newborns. And with a $6.7 billion budget, it is well-financed, until you consider that its budget is less than 7 percent of what we have to spend on substance abuse in the workplace.

● The federal school lunch program also has a large budget, estimated at $12.4 billion in 2006—which is just a little less than vandals cost us every year. Feed a kid for a month, or paint "Arnie Was Here" on the side of a building. You would think the choice would be obvious.

● Last year, Congress provided almost $208 million in funding for libraries, a budget that was roughly one-eighth of what we spent for bioterrorism preparations.

● The federal budget in 2005 to provide special education for homeless children is $62.5 million, or about one-third less than we spent just fighting human traffickers.

● The federal child literacy program has a budget of $1.2 billion this year, which sounds like a lot until you consider it is less than 3 percent of what we spent dealing with drunk drivers.

● In fact, the entire budget for the U.S. Department of Education is $71.5 billion this year, or 25 percent less than we spend just combating healthcare fraud.

Living Healthier and Happier. Former President Jimmy Carter has been a terrific advocate for Habitat For Humanity, a volunteer organization that builds homes for people who otherwise could not have their own homes. And with a budget of $162 million in 2004, Habitat does terrific work. What a shame that in Southern California, they spend that much every couple months prosecuting gang murders.

The National Cancer Institute is at the forefront of cancer research and prevention. However, its big budget of $4.9 billion this year is approximately 1 percent of what we spent on the tort system. Certainly, I am not advocating eliminating the tort system, but I worry more about cancer than I do about winning a 44-cent refund on my cable service because the cable company incorrectly billed me and two million others four years ago.

The Center for Disease Control is one of our most crucial federal agencies, and we should be happy the government funds it to the tune of $7.7 billion this year. Unfortunately, that is only about 4 percent of what we spend fighting drug abuse. What a shame we have to devote such massive resources to addicts turning cold medicines into death drugs, as opposed to beating the natural epidemics that ravage mankind.

Worldwide Helping Programs—The Big Numbers. In fact, take a look at what we spent on all these other crucial programs and departments:

- The Peace Corps—$317 million

- Library of Congress—$559 million

- National Endowment for the Arts—$101 million

- The National Park Foundation—$48 million

- U.S. Consumer Product Safety Commission—$65 million

And add in a few really, really big budgets:

- U.S. tsunami aid as of July 2005—$1.7 billion

- Total U.S. foreign aid estimated in 2006—$9.1 billion

And the total for all the above would be about 2 percent of what we spend during the same period *just on white-collar crime and workplace fraud!*

WHAT IF WE ELIMINATED OR REDUCED THE WEASEL TAX?

Once you begin to lay out these numbers, the enormous potential of a Weasel-free society (or at least a society with substantially fewer Weasels) becomes apparent. Imagine how much better your life could be if your taxes fell by 50–75 percent (assuming you're not a Weasel who doesn't pay taxes). Sound too good to be true? Well, the numbers add up quickly. Just look at a few:

- "Tax surcharge" on the average taxpayer due to those who don't pay their taxes—15 percent

- Amount average taxpayer pays for tort system—$845

- Average cost per worker of white-collar crime—$4,500

- Average cost per person for bankruptcies—$400

Now of course we won't ever totally eliminate tax cheats, white-collar crime, the tort system, or bankruptcies, but imagine if we reduced them by 25 percent. Depending on your tax bracket, if you and your spouse both work, this could easily mean an additional $5,000 or more per year in your pocket!

And that's just the tip of the iceberg: imagine if we were able to get the same reductions in healthcare fraud and white-collar crime! Because companies will save on Weasel costs, they will be more competitive and be able to expand, they will be able to pay employees more, and they will be able to distribute more to stockholders in capital gains and increase in value.

And then the trickle-down economic theory really begins to sing, with everyone moving up an economic notch or two. And not only will you have more to spend, but reducing Weasel infestation will lower prices, as companies pass on savings and become more competitive. And this means a U.S. economy that becomes more competitive with foreign economies that have formerly had an edge on us because they have not had to implement such extensive Weasel-protection policies. And life in general becomes easier, too. Weasel protection is not only expensive; it is time consuming and annoying.

BUT IS IT POSSIBLE TO ELIMINATE THE WEASEL TAX?

Reducing the Weasel tax seems daunting, if not impossible, but consider the following facts of how Weasel behavior has proliferated in recent years.

Our tax system encourages Weasels. Many Weasel taxes we now pay did not exist a decade or a generation ago. For instance, as our tax structure has grown more complicated, so has the potential and incentive for abuse. In fact, we did not even have federal taxes until my father's generation. Cleaning up the tax structure and making tax cheats pay could immediately generate hundreds of millions in revenue. We need to make our politicians and governmental agencies accountable to taxpayers, and not the massive corporations that are finding loopholes to avoid paying taxes.

Our bankruptcy and tort systems encourage Weasels. Our recent liberal bankruptcy and tort laws (and settlements) are encouraging Weasel behavior at an alarming rate. Our overtaxed and complex legal system and the Weasel legal structure it has spawned are a recent phenomenon. When people took more responsibility for their actions, they didn't feel inclined to turn to the courts anytime something went wrong.

Our love of big business encourages Weasels. The rise of the megacorporation has increased the size of white-collar crime via the sheer enormity of the thefts, e.g., Enron and Worldcom. Although America has (and should remain) an intensely capitalistic society, we have more recently become infatuated with the "CEO as rock star"—resulting in a breed of business managers who have lived above the law (and thankfully, now many of them are living in eight-by-ten cells).

Our attitudes toward drugs encourage Weasels. Our increasingly liberal (and expensive) approach toward addiction is a massive financial burden we are all shouldering. When we made the societal switch from "addiction is a choice you made, and if you want to help yourself, we will help you get better" to "addiction is a societal disease that chose you and we must all pay for it," we began paying a much bigger tax and encouraging addiction.

Part of the problem is also our inability to separate punishment for addiction from punishing the Weasels who spawn addiction. We have more Americans in prison than any time in history—primarily due to drugs—which is an expensive societal tax. Many of those in prison should be in less expensive treatment, and we should devote the saved resources to prosecuting the big Weasels who create and distribute the really heinous drugs. Regardless of your feelings about "gateway drugs," if you have limited resources, it also makes much more sense to put away big crystal meth distributors as opposed to someone caught with a big baggie of pot.

And what if, instead of taxing society for the choices a few make, we all fully paid for our own choices? If you want to smoke, that is your choice, but pay $12 for a pack of cigarettes so I don't have to pay for your choice via my taxes and lost productivity. I enjoy a cocktail or a glass or two of wine, so I and others who drink should be willing to pay more for the right and the problems it incurs via increased liquor taxes as opposed those who never touch a drop. Remember: RIGHTS = RESPONSIBILITY.

And the liquor companies that make fortified wines that are purely targeted at late-stage alcoholics should have to price accordingly to the true cost that is incurred as a result of this wine. If fortified wines cost the same as a fine Pinot Noir, I think the market would shift.

Warriors accept the responsibility and the blame. I suspect if those responsible paid the true cost of their habits and addictions, we would have many fewer addicts.

Our society in the U.S. encourages Weasels. Precedents have been set by other current societies. Many of the problems we suffer from in the U.S. are not problems in other similar countries. For instance, the tremendous cost we pay for gun violence does not exist in Canada, a society similar to ours. Canada also places many limitations on the size of lawsuits, and they have a much more simplistic legal system. As I have found on my visits to Japan, theft, gun violence, and many other crimes that plague the U.S. are almost nonexistent. So our problems are not genetic—they are social, and accordingly we can change.

SO HOW DO WE START TO FIGHT
THE WEASEL TAX?

In his bestseller *The Tipping Point: How Little Things Can Make A Big Difference*, author Malcolm Gladwell demonstrates how major social shifts can occur based on small grassroots changes. He points out that New York City experienced a massive decrease in crime in the 1990s. Over a five-year period, murders decreased an astounding 64.3 percent, and total crime fell by almost 50 percent. New York went from being one of the most dangerous cities in the world to one of the safest, in just a few short years. As a result, the trickle-down effect occurred: tourism jumped, the economy drastically improved, civic pride took a huge increase, and the overall quality of life in New York improved radically.

Although experts have offered many different explanations for this phenomenon, one approach that Gladwell points to that had a huge impact was a city-wide program to start *by attacking small crimes*:

● Vandalism was no longer tolerated.

● The city's subways were cleaned up, run more professionally, and kept clean.

● Police presence was increased, and petty crime was suddenly taken seriously. Police took a hard stance against minor crimes such as jumping the subway fare turnstyles, vagrancy, and theft. Basically, they cracked down on even petty Weasel behavior.

And the result? All crime decreased. Attitudes changed, and things got better.

So what would happen if American society embarked on a major program to reduce Weasel behavior? Forty-five years ago, John F. Kennedy announced to America that we would be the first nation to travel to the moon when the idea seemed a bit ludicrous, but we achieved it. Reducing Weasel behavior by 25 percent would seem to be a much easier task to achieve than conquering another planet!

Imagine if our president announced a program to reduce the Weasel tax by 25 percent over the next five years. I suspect this would be a much easier sell than the various Social Security changes currently being debated, as this would mean immediate savings to taxpayers, and an increase in their quality of life. And wouldn't it be terrific if for once this program had bipartisan support? After all, what kind of politician wouldn't support an anti-Weasel campaign? (Perhaps a Weasel politician?) The program would probably consist of a few of the following components.

Improve education. Forty years ago, with a teary-eyed Native American as its spokesman, the federal government educated us all about littering, and our highways and streets immediately became a lot cleaner. Let's educate people not to act like Weasels. People are tremendously impacted by the media: what if we released a major advertising campaign promoting ethical behavior and making Weasel behavior absolutely unacceptable?

Reduce Weasel incentives. Change the ridiculous and complex laws that promote Weasel behavior. Simplify the tax code to eliminate shady tax dodges. Make moves to reduce needless litigation, and punish the Weasel attorneys who promote such actions. We already made a move to tighten the loose bankruptcy laws, so we've taken the first step; let's keep going.

Increase prosecution of Weasel criminals. We've taken the first steps by putting some of our biggest white-collar Weasels in prison; let's step up the enforcement.

As New Yorkers experienced ten years ago, small steps can lead to big gains. A concerted effort by all of us to reduce the Weasel tax could be a major boon to society.

· · · · · · · · · · ·

In the next and final section of the book, we will wrap up the Four W's with a few final thoughts about how this philosophy may best fit into your life.

PART SIX

Wrapping Up

WRAPPING UP

Love Yourself— Just Not Too Much: Walking the Fine Line Between Healthy Self-Confidence and a Destructive Ego

---

"I never wanted to be famous, just good."
—Ray Charles

One of the consistent issues intertwined throughout the world of *Warriors, Workers, Whiners, and Weasels* is ego management. This is a tough one. Warriors must be filled with self-confidence and have hefty egos, but if they grow too large or unrealistic they may go the way of the Weasel. Workers who have the talent and tools and aspire to be Warriors may need a bit of an ego infusion, or they could achieve a higher degree of happiness if they just loved themselves as much as they deserve to be loved. Whiners typically suffer from low self-esteem; if they could capture the necessary self-confidence—and perhaps love themselves a bit more—they would be happier and live life as a Worker or Warrior.

Loving yourself just enough for the right reasons, but not too much becomes the key.

I've met many individuals who have never progressed in their social lives or careers primarily because their ego does not allow them to foster normal human relationships. They are so focused on themselves that they never develop their relationship tools.

Those who achieve success often develop a different set of ego-related issues. As you grow more successful, the balancing act becomes increasingly difficult, because it is challenging to keep one's ego intact when everyone around you is feeding it for his or her own motivations, or even because you really do deserve the accolades. "Believing one's own press" is seldom advisable (something I can personally attest to). My business involves working with a lot of celebrities who run the gamut from legendary to "yeah, wasn't he the guy in . . .?" One of the biggest problems the famous face is finding a way to keep a real-world perspective when their own lives are so far from the real world. I know that, in my own life, I am constantly disappointing myself when I let my ego get out of control, yet it is also easy to fall into depression when you allow yourself to become overly self-critical.

In many ways, people can be classified by the state of their ego at any given time, and usually, as someone progresses through life and experiences failures and successes, they gain maturity and their ego naturally progresses and refines to an acceptable level that suits them well. Possessing the ability to assess and control your own self-confidence level, and the impact of it on those around you, is a valuable tool.

One of the most common statements people make when reminiscing about past phases of their lives is "if I only knew then what I know now." I have found that, in most cases, the literal translation of that statement really is "if I had only had the confidence then that I have now." Most people who say this suffered through one or more of the following: the pain of childhood shyness, the need to be accepted, the awkwardness of adolescence, confrontations with the neighborhood bully, fear of trying out for a sports team or club, envy of the "cool kids" who they watched from afar as they wished they could be part of the group.

And if they weathered these storms, within a few short years, these uncomfortable experiences seem trite and unimportant. Most of us come to realize that most bullies are more myth than reality. Often the "cool kids" didn't even realize they were in the revered crowd, and falling from grace comes easily. In time, we usually come to understand that if we failed to make the proper moves in our youthful days, all we really lacked was the self-confidence to proclaim ourselves one of the "cool kids," to stand up to the bully, to play more aggressively on the team (and perhaps become the hero of the day), or to ask that special person to the dance.

Though we constantly make these realizations, many people fail to carry this lesson forward. Once they get into the workplace or a new social situation, they repeat the cycles of their youth, failing to aggressively pursue what they really want because of a lack of confidence, and then lamenting their lack of progress. Sadly, a decade or two down the road, they often wake up to realize they missed their true goals, repeating a pattern they set early in life. They constantly choose the safe road instead of pursuing their real dreams. They never escape their fear of the "mythical bully," and they relegate themselves to never becoming a part of the group they really want to belong to, or more aptly put, to achieve what they dream of achieving. Sometimes, this results in bitterness that further clouds their lives, transforming them into Whiners or worse, or often they just settle in.

Of course, there is nothing wrong with happily settling in and finding contentment and satisfaction in what you are doing. In fact, it is the ultimate goal that many never achieve. But living life dissatisfied because of the mythical bully is a shame, and the person who chooses to live this way can only blame himself or herself. It is your responsibility to take the control.

Certainly, there is nothing wrong with enjoying the fruits of your success, and we all deserve the right to crow a bit about our success. But there is a way to handle it all respectfully. Success is a great addition to your personal brand, and it can also enhance your relationship tool. But the successful manage to keep their egos in check, and they maintain a natural curiosity about others that helps them to keep achieving.

Ultimately, we all face the challenge of the *balance*. We need to be realistic about our strong and weak points, love ourselves, and have the confidence to go anywhere we want to go while constantly working to improve in those areas that need improvement—without taking it too far and letting our ego destroy us. Loving yourself, and feeling comfortable within your own skin for all the right reasons is a great goal.

. . . .

In the next and final chapter, we will see what achieving this goal is all about.

CHAPTER 22

Enjoy the Ride,
or The Lesson You Should
Really Learn From This Book

"You only live once, but if you live life like me, **once is enough.**"
— Frank Sinatra

s I move (sometimes kicking and screaming) into middle age, I constantly come to terms with the mistakes I have made, and continue to make. Luckily, they have not been major life-threatening mistakes, but mistakes that have resulted in me enjoying life just a little less than I would have preferred; they've made me appreciate all that I possess less than I should. Certainly, that is an experience most of us share.

This has often been the result of encounters with Weasels, incorrect use of my Warrior tools, and my own missteps.

But perhaps this should also ultimately lead to a discussion of the big goal. If you bought this book to tune your Warrior skills, have you thought about why do you want to be a Warrior? Is it that you crave power, success, and/or money? Do you want a great big Warrior car or custom Warrior Harley? A Warrior jet? Your name on top of a building? Are there people in your life you feel a need to prove something to? Is it because you believe Warriors have more sex with more attractive people than you do?

Is it ingrained and you just can't help it? All of the above? What should the ultimate goal really be?

Using my Warrior's tools to the best of my ability has served me well, as has limiting my exposure to Weasels. I have achieved much of what I set out to achieve for the place I am at, and I look forward to new and more interesting goals to conquer. I have a great wife, family, friends, financial security, a terrific business that has allowed me to work with some incredibly talented people, and I'm fairly pleased with my personal brand. And now I want to take the next step forward—which actually means taking a step backwards. I want to be as smart as I was when I was twelve.

I have come to realize that it is incorrect to assume that as you get older, you automatically get smarter about everything. Certainly, with experience you get smarter about most things. But I was smarter about a few important things at the age of twelve than I am now. At twelve, I could spend an entire afternoon immersed in the fantasies of my future: the wonderful adventures that were going to happen in my life. Now, I spend too many afternoons concentrating on silly minutia that really doesn't matter, ranging from a squeak in my car to the bad service I received at a restaurant.

When I was twelve, the best dinner in the world cost a buck and a half, came from A&W, and was topped off by a root beer float. Now, I sometimes need to mentally slap myself when I find myself complaining that the radicchio in my $14 salad is wilting, or my wine has been decanted improperly.

When I was twelve, I could meet a new guy in the neighborhood, and within two hours, we would be playing baseball without a care in the world, both pleased with the fact that we had a new best friend. Too often, now I spend inordinate amounts of time analyzing the motivations of anyone who attempts to form a relationship with me, utilizing my Weasel radar, always harboring the unfortunately often-justified fear that their true motivation is to just get something from me.

When I was twelve, almost everything had the potential to be magical. Time moved slowly and allowed me to luxuriate in the moment. I was unburdened by possessions, and because I had met few Weasels, I was eternally optimistic.

Now my goal is to stay a Warrior and continue to hone my Warrior skills, *but also to adopt certain attributes and attitudes of a twelve-year-old.* No matter how old I become, I want to dream with great anticipation of all the wonderful adventures and people I might meet. I want to look forward to what might happen that will still amaze me. I want to keep my cynicism and the bad memories of my Weasel encounters in check (otherwise, the Weasels win), and I want to overcome my frequent silly impatience and anger. My final advice to all of us is this:

- Find a new friend and play baseball (literally or figuratively).

- Stay up late, put aside reality for a little while, and watch a silly, scary movie.

- Call up someone on the phone you haven't spoken to in a long time (a non-Weasel) and reminisce for an hour or two. Choose someone with whom you can safely let your guard down. Have the kind of open and honest conversation you haven't had since you were twelve.

- Every now and then, take a "snow day," a well-deserved day off when you can lie around, take a walk, or see a movie matinee.

- Go dancing.

- Eat a chocolate chip cookie without feeling guilty.

- Don't let the Weasels get you down.

Although I can't predict the future, I can guarantee that some day, when you look back on it all, your only regret will be that you didn't enjoy the ride more. See you on the playground!

INDEX